'THESE ARE ENERGISED FEELINGS THAT CAN SPARK REVOLUTIONS'

– Jessica Brough, page 19

NEW TESTIMONIALS

NEW TESTIMONIALS

NEW TESTIMONIALS

Published in the UK in 2019 by
Monstrous Regiment Publishing Ltd.
Edinburgh, Scotland
editor@monstrous-regiment.com
www.monstrous-regiment.com

Distributed in the UK by
Monstrous Regiment Publishing Ltd.

ISBN: 978-1-9161179-1-4

Printed and bound in Great Britain by Clays Ltd, Elcograf S.p.A.

NEW TESTIMONIALS

NEW TESTIMONIALS

NEW TESTIMONIALS

NEW TESTIMONIALS

NEW TESTIMONIALS

NEW TESTIMONIALS

**Further original narratives
and essays about bisexuality**

Foreword by Kemah Bob
Edited by Lauren Nickodemus & Ellen Desmond

EDITORS' NOTE

In 2017, our newly born micropress decided to launch *The Bi-ble*, a collection of essays about the experience of being bisexual and occupying a liminal and often erased space. We didn't know what to expect, but we knew we wanted to at least try to get our book and its message out into the world. With the help of over 200 Kickstarter backers, we produced and printed a small run of the first volume and soon began to realize just how much need and hunger there was for bisexual stories and content. We couldn't keep up. It took 293 more Kickstarter backers of these editions in 2019 to help us meet the demand.

The reaction to *The Bi-ble* from readers who told us how much it had inspired and validated them encouraged us to continue sharing the experiences of our community. At first we considered extending the original book with just a few extra pieces, but quickly found that there were so many stories and perspectives we wanted to share that a whole new standalone volume was warranted. It also meant past readers wouldn't have to rebuy Volume One in order to access the new stories.

As we said in the original *Bi-ble*, we know we'll never be able to share every bisexual+ experience. But we began work on *Volume 2: New Testimonials* in summer 2018 in the hopes our duo of books would wedge themselves in on bookshelves and claim some much-deserved visible space for the often erased B in LGBTQ+. Producing Volume Two has been an exciting and, at times, cathartic and challenging experience. To be able to bring these writers' wonderful pieces to you is a once in a lifetime opportunity and it has meant the world to us. The essays in this book are powerful, honest, and so important. We hope that they resonate with you and help you feel seen, valid, and loved – as they have often made us feel seen, valid and loved.

On a personal note, these books hold a special place in our hearts not just as editors and publishers, but as bisexuals ourselves. One story that is secretly written in these pages and the pages of The Bi-ble is how we fell in love while researching Volume One and, what's more, found a community and identity where we finally felt accepted and at home. We hope these books come to mean something really special to you too.

Ellen Desmond
Lauren Nickodemus
May 2019

CONTENTS

PLEASE NOTE

We would like to alert readers that some essays contain potentially triggering content, particularly in the areas of biphobia and homophobia, painful outings or coming-outs, as well as identity erasure and accounts of facing prejudice or discrimination.

The following essays also include mentions of:

Sexual assault and rape
You, You and I by Arthur Walsh, page 77
Tapestries Woven in Many Threads by Rosalind Smith, page 115
A Man, a Cane, an Awkward Title by Sandra Alland, page 151

Childhood abuse
You, You and I by Arthur Walsh, page 77
A Man, a Cane, an Awkward Title by Sandra Alland, page 151

Violence or assault
How Louisa May Alcott Helped Me to Survive Being Outed
by Jo Landon, page 141

FOREWORD

by Kemah Bob

Last August I took part in a live recording of *The Guilty Feminist* in Edinburgh, themed around invisibility. In our discussion of invisibility we couldn't go long without touching on bi visibility and bi-erasure. Bi-erasure might be an all too familiar term to many of us, but you'd be surprised how many people still don't know it's an issue and how important it is to have these conversations.

As fate would have it, in the crowd that day was Monstrous Regiment, who approached me afterwards to ask if I'd be down to get involved with this project. The idea of writing a foreword for a book was pretty intimidating, but I would not and could not miss the opportunity to be a part of the voices featured in this anthology.

I feel like within the queer community the lack of respect for the bisexual identity can be even worse. Sometimes people still look down on us, even when we're going down on them!

As a pansexual woman who's formerly identified as bisexual… I find the two terms to mean the exact same thing. While I don't think bisexuality is in itself exclusionary, I do feel some interpretations of the word can be. The dictionary definition of bisexual includes 'attracted to both men and women' leaving out people that identify as neither altogether. The definition for pansexual includes 'not limited in sexual choice'. Which I find hilarious. I for one draw my sexual limit at straight cisgender white men. It's not that I haven't. Oh I have, and I have had enough.

I'm also tired of the pressure to appear to be queer; when as queer people *any* way we present is by default queer. What does it even mean to be queer? Where do definitions and labels stop serving to empower us and begin to box us in? When do they begin to limit the ways we think we're entitled to feel about ourselves and other people?

In 'I Still Feel Like I Can't Quite Be Myself' (page 63) Jayna Tavarez discusses pressures on bisexual role models and activist burnout, which is a discussion of her thesis findings showing how the emotional labour of representing an identity is often exhausting for those trying to stand up and do their best. The writers in this book have put themselves out there as activists in their own way too. They've chosen to represent the bi umbrella or describe how they've looked for representation in a multitude of ways; in the ways they know best.

For Jessica Brough on page 19 it was at a Janelle Monáe gig where she found her 'existence in that space ... concrete and unapologetic.' Likewise, other writers in this book have found themselves or created an image of themselves in movies, at gigs, through their own writing or in novels. Some simply discuss not finding bi representation anywhere.

On stage, I joke that I left Texas for California after university to 'catch up on all the gay I'd missed,' and though Los Angeles was the most liberal state I've ever lived in, it was London where I would finally feel comfortable owning my sexuality. A huge part of that was finally being welcomed into the queer nightlife scene by my fairy gay-mother Aisha, and through The Cocoa Butter Club, began performing at events within the community.

Sometimes, in some places it feels like things have improved greatly for marginalised folk, but other days it feels like we've not gotten very far at all. For many bisexuals, like Vaneet Mehta on page 9, coming out will be 'the hardest thing he's ever had to do.' I for one am not out to half of my family who – sorry Monstrous Regiment – will hopefully not read this book.

Though I've physically left Texas, I haven't been able to escape all the pain of rejection from home. It was only last Christmas when my best friend told me she 'can't accept what the Creator deems abominable' and hopes to see me return to the 'natural law'. I've used quotation marks because those are fucking quotes.

Yet, here I am in London. Living out my dreams in the largest, loveliest queer community I've ever seen or felt. It's a privilege to be able to flee persecution. To be a part of an attempt to create spaces where people of every gender and sexuality can feel safe. Because the reality is not everywhere is safe; acknowledge your privilege.

We can all do better to educate ourselves and be allies. Ally is a term that's often overused and under fulfilled. Of course we as members of the LGBTQ+ community know this, but still we have blind spots we aren't always conscious of. I encourage you to interrogate where and most importantly how you can better support others.

And celebrate. Celebrate your life; celebrate your truth and bask in your queerness. Whatever that means to you.

Kemah Bob
May 2019

BIDENTITY

by Rebecca Wojturska

TO BEGIN BLUNTLY, I am a bisexual who has never slept with a woman.

I start with this disclaimer because sometimes using the term bisexual for myself can feel like the wrong fit, like trying on someone else's well-worn clothes and wondering if the shape isn't quite right. Since I first came out, in gauging the reactions of those I told and foraying into the world of online dating, I've felt that emphasis is often placed on the 'sexual' aspect of the label. Consequently, due to my semi-virginal status, I have often (a) questioned my place within the queer community and (b) felt erased, and therefore uncomfortable, within the straight community. This has been enhanced by the fact that I have since settled down with a heterosexual male.

So why am I writing about bisexuality? Probably because I feel like I've been living in a liminal world, not gay and not straight, unable to fully relax with either label. And though my position must be far from unique, it's not one I've encountered very often at all. Narrative space has, rightfully so, been predominantly given to those who have struggled with the stigma of coming out. But the space is widening, and to understand queerness we need to understand the experiences of people across the entire queer spectrum.

It's not difficult to guess why someone wouldn't come out until they're 25. It started, as it usually does, with witnessing homophobia at a young age. I was eight when a rumour spread round our primary school that someone was a lesbian. Everyone stopped speaking to this girl and were cruel behind her back, as if fancying girls was something dirty and you could catch it. Meanwhile, the playground was thronging with positively reinforced straight 'crushes': fake weddings, connecting with your friends through gossiping and the giggling rush of admitting you fancied a boy in your class. The separation of gender at such a young age meant that to admit having a crush on someone on your side of the border meant to be exiled, deemed untrustworthy. I know now that I took two unexamined beliefs away from this: that finding girls attractive was bad, and that you should never tell anyone if you do.

Sadly, this mindset is not found only on the playground. Adults can of course be just as cruel, with varying degrees of influence or inclination to say hateful things. By denying my bisexuality I evaded the hurtful and often life-damaging stigma that can come with being open about who you are, but my mental health suffered. Depression, anxiety and an eating disorder were fuelled by suppression. When my sister came out as gay, I was very happy for two reasons. One: she had lived a confused childhood and received no support where her sexuality was concerned, so to see her take ownership over something we had all somehow recognised was amazing – she was more comfortable with her identity than we had ever seen. Two: I finally knew someone who was out and proud. As my sister got girlfriends I got jealous, yet still I didn't tell anyone. Why? I felt that without a girlfriend I wasn't actually bisexual. I told myself I would announce it to the world once I'd met someone. However, I wasn't putting myself out there or in situations where I would *actually* meet someone. So, I ended up with men every time – something I found easier and, to be honest, less scary. It turned out I was only comfortable entering the unknown if it involved the ghosts and sinister figures between the pages of a Gothic novel.

My first foray into acting on this aspect of my sexuality was getting drunk in nightclubs and asking women that I found beautiful if they were attracted to women. (What a chat-up line.) I do not recommend this approach. My friends' reaction on hearing me do this was to call me weird. I know, right? I laughed along with them, more than embarrassed of myself. No one asked me if I was attracted to women. I don't think they wanted to know and, to some extent, neither did I.

But it came out. Strangely, the first person I told was my ex-boyfriend in 2013, because I had just cheated on him with a woman at a nightclub. And no, it wasn't one of my drunk, terrible excuses for a chat-up line that did it (although I *was* drunk). While I was dancing with my friends to indie music, a woman approached me. We chatted and danced, then she leaned in to kiss me. I shouldn't have welcomed it, but my drunken self didn't flag up the moral issue. The kiss didn't last long. I heard a friend scream my name in shock, which brought me back to reality. I left her and went to the bar. What is worse, I pretended that I was just as shocked as my friends were. I felt terrible about kissing someone while in a relationship with someone else. But something had been liberated in me. I had finally kissed a girl and I not only liked it, I loved it.

Telling my ex-boyfriend was tough. He was angry that someone else had hit on me, but I suspected it would have been worse if it had been a man. I decided to tell him I was attracted to women. Waiting for anger, hurt and misunderstanding, I was shocked when he immediately suggested a threesome.

From what I've read or heard, this is not an uncommon reaction, and it wasn't the last time I heard it. The implication that women's pleasure should always somehow serve a man's seems to be a widely held belief. It seems to be another reason people feel they can't be honest about their bisexuality. Because there's always the threat that someone can take something away from it – that it will always be pulled into the realms of and subordinated to heterosexual male gratification.

Other reactions I've had to my coming out have been just as disparaging. In the spirit of open discussion, someone asked me whether or not I might like women because they are sexualised so much in general (an unfounded and unfair anxiety I've sadly had myself, and another reason for my reluctance in coming out). Much more commonly, people have said, 'Oh, but you've found your boyfriend now,' as if he saved me from my lost wanderings of confusion in the Forest of Bi. As if I only wanted to experiment with women while waiting for 'the (male) one'.

Apart from my current boyfriend, ex-partners have feared that I will leave them for a woman – a surprising, lopsided fear, given that I'd be no less likely to leave them for a man. But something about bisexuality can leave people feeling uneasy, as though your ability to love and lust after anyone, irrespective of gender, means you are more likely to jump between partners. That even after you've settled down, your sexuality remains a live threat, some dangerous fire. Lastly, among reactions there has been gross misunderstanding. Even as recently as last month, someone, to my face, albeit extremely drunkenly, compared homosexuality to paedophilia.

However, my family were generally supportive. A few lacklustre 'okays', my sister telling me she suspected all along, and my mother being excited for me made me feel like a burden was lifted. Not the burden of my sexuality, but the burden of disallowing myself to explore it. I decided to – deep breath – join dating websites. Anecdotally, my current partner, who was my close friend at the time, helped me set up my profiles. He helped me take and pick pictures, write my bio and, most importantly, offered a judgement-free space to talk. Between him and my mother, who constantly asked if I'd met someone yet (which was far from being patronising or intrusive for me at that time), I felt excited to be finally putting myself out there in a sober and adult way.

Imagine my disappointment when there were about three local lesbians/bisexuals on Match.com and a few handfuls of lesbians/bisexuals on Tinder. Bios on dating apps are brutal. Most of them explicitly rejected bisexuals, some only wanted phone sex (one way the app can be used, but something I wasn't after) and some weren't interested (fair enough). But lo and behold, I had a few matches! And I didn't even have to think of something clever-but-also-relatable-but-also-funny to say first. The messages that popped up in my inbox read:

- Are you bi or lesbian?
- Have you ever slept with a woman before?
- Are you new to the gay scene?
- What underwear are you wearing?

This was intimidating for me (and not just because I wear boring pants). I thought we would open with a pretentious quote from a favourite author or perhaps a pun so bad it's hilarious. But I soon realised that quickly establishing your identity in the community was important on the apps. But for someone who didn't know, and to some extent still doesn't know, where they fit in the community, this can feel rough. Each woman's impatience at my sexual reticence and inexperience made me feel further alienated and, to be honest, a bit angry. *I have more to offer*, I would bitterly think (but I've since realised that if you're after something that someone isn't offering, there is no sense leading them on). That said, even if two people knew exactly who they were and what they wanted, they still wouldn't know whether or not a date would work out. But one whiff of an inexperienced bisexual and women were running as if I were the Ghost of Pre-sexual Past.

A major positive I did draw from dating apps was seeing women be completely honest with what they wanted, whether that was hooking up or not. But I was looking for friendships and I wanted to see if any would blossom. I made friends who had some of the same interests as me – The Beatles, Bowie, vegetarianism, Gothic books, more Gothic books – but grew sad as they told me they met someone and phased me out. I felt like I was too slow. Feeling the sting of lesbians who wouldn't even consider me, sadness that someone only wanted to talk dirty to me (which is great, unless you're not interested) and self-doubt about my attractiveness meant I slowly abandoned the dating apps. They can work for some, but for those less confident, like me, they can leave you feeling empty.

It wasn't long after this experience that I began a relationship with my current partner, who had helped me explore the apps in the first place. We now live together and are settling in for the long haul. People often assume that if you're attracted to both men and women, then to be with only one means you're satisfying only part of your desire. Bullshit. Another common assumption is that settling down with one extinguishes any possibility of finding the other(s) attractive. Bullshit. Being happy in a monogamous relationship with a man means that I could easily stay silent about my bisexuality, but I'm not comfortable with that. There's no reason to pretend I'm straight and I'll continue to voice my experience when it's relevant and needed.

Some people seem to think that I must have some 'unfinished business' with women and that my bisexuality will lead me back to them inevitably. But this is a harmful misunderstanding and I shouldn't feel like I have to prove myself. My sexual activity does not negate my sexual identity (or, as a friend put it, it's in the attraction, not the action). Being attracted to women without ever having sex with one makes me feel like the word bisexual doesn't quite cut it (especially as the 'sex' part hasn't played out for me). But I know of no better word, and so that's exactly who I am: a bisexual who has never had sex with a woman. And the only unfinished business I have is building the rest of my life with my love.

THE HARDEST THING I'VE EVER HAD TO DO

by Vaneet Mehta

COMING OUT AS bisexual was one of the hardest things I've ever had to do. For as long as I can remember, there has been something not 'right' about me. I always see people put down a single moment where they realised they weren't straight, but I can't recall one. I can't even put an age on it. But I do know that it happened before I even entered high school. I remember having crushes on girls in my year, wanting to date them or kiss them. But along with this, I also remember a weird curiosity inside of me about the guys in my year. I always wanted to see more of them. This sensation always felt wrong to me, probably for several reasons.

Growing up in a British Asian household in a densely populated Asian area in the 90s was not an easy task. I've always found the British Asian culture to be suffocating. Indian traditions, which naturally feed British Asian culture, are very regressive and enforce strict gender roles. This can be seen very clearly through our media, such as Bollywood movies where over-muscled male protagonists have to protect the overtly feminine leading lady. I even see it in our family households; the women always tend to cook and clean and look after the children, whilst the men work and not much else. This ideology is ingrained into us and constantly reinforced.

Many people within my culture expect everyone to be carbon copies of one another; to like the same things, talk the same, act the same. My school mostly consisted of people from the British Asian community and it felt like they were one big clique. Because I was different from them, I was an outcast. I was constantly labelled a coconut, brown on the outside and white on the inside. I didn't like the same music, play the same games, or act anything like my peers. This last part is the biggest issue people in my culture have with me. Whilst I am not overtly feminine, I am pretty far removed from what is considered masculine. I don't work out, I don't talk or act like a lad, I don't play FIFA or *Call of Duty*. In fact, I am a very emotional person who loves collecting soft toys. This is met with a lot of opposition.

My dad used to constantly belittle me, asking me, 'Why don't you look like the other guys?' and, 'When will you stop being such a girl?' I was called gay by plenty of people growing up. In the 90s, 'gay' had become a synonym for bad. I'm not proud of the fact that even I used it that way. I don't think I realised, not at first, that it planted the idea in my head that there was something wrong with being homosexual. I was constantly opposed to being called gay, and it damaged my psyche while I was questioning my sexuality. Connecting my homosexual thoughts to something negative made me push them away.

Representation also played into this. Gay people in media were always very stereotypical. They were always into fashion or dancing or make-up. I always looked at this and thought that that's what it meant to be gay. Since I couldn't relate to that, I thought, 'Well, I can't be gay then,' and pushed my feelings to one side. An even bigger issue was the complete lack of bisexual representation.

Looking back, I can't ever recall bisexuality being part of the internal conversation I was having in my head. All I can remember is me asking myself, 'Am I gay or am I straight?' I was never informed of any other options, like bisexual. I constantly swung between the two, crushing on a girl and then finding a guy attractive. I didn't know what that meant and couldn't explain it with anything I had been taught, which made things confusing.

The first instance I can remember where bisexuality became apparent was in Sixth Form. Someone had come out as bicurious, saying she was into men but curious about women. I remember hearing this and a lightbulb going off in my head, thinking this explained my own feelings. However, this was quickly shut down. People were laughing at this, saying, 'Who is she kidding?', invalidating bicurious as a thing. I'm ashamed to say I played into it. For all I knew, maybe it was just made up. I had never heard of it until that point. Every now and then, bicurious came up in my internal conversation, but never for long, as I just couldn't see it as valid. I knew others wouldn't either, so there was no use in voicing these thoughts. I knew everyone would just label me as gay.

In fact, I saw this myself. When I was at university, I was watching an episode of 90210 with my housemate. In the episode, they revealed that Teddy had slept with a man whilst drunk. My housemate immediately labelled him as gay. I reminded her that Teddy had had previous relationships with multiple women in the show, so he could be bisexual or bicurious. She disagreed with me on this, saying that there was no coming back after sleeping with a man, so he must be gay. It made it worse that 90210 went down this route as well, painting it as a 'gay-in-denial' storyline. Whilst 'gay-in-denial' is a valid situation that happens to many people in the real world, it always feels like a bisexual storyline is never considered. The constant bi-erasure in media was a huge issue for me. Since bisexual was never seen as a valid sexuality, I constantly denied who I was.

I ended up repressing my sexuality for a very long time. Whilst I had sexual urges for men, I couldn't envision myself having sex with a man as – to put it politely – the 'logistics' involved concerned me. I also couldn't envision being in a relationship with a man. I found it extremely difficult to connect with any men, even in my own family. Most of my closest friends were, and still are, women. Calling myself straight felt wrong; I knew I was probably bicurious (maybe a one or two on the Kinsey Scale), but I was too anxious to explore any of these feelings. This all changed when I fell in love with my straight best friend.

When I first met him, we didn't entirely get on. We had similar interests and a lot of great conversations, but disagreed on a few things. Over the course of a couple of years, we grew a lot closer and became best friends. I didn't have any feelings for him, sexual or romantic, during that time. I'm not sure how, and I'm not sure when, but one day something changed. I struggled with this a lot, constantly denying the feelings that I had now grown for him. However, we were best friends and that meant we spent a lot of time together. The more time I spent with him, the deeper these feelings grew. And the deeper they grew, the more work I had to do to deny them. The more I denied them, the more damage I caused to my psyche.

I struggled with this for over a year until it finally hit a head at the end of 2016. I couldn't go on denying my feelings for him anymore and, with that, I could no longer deny my sexuality. I knew I had to speak to someone about it, so I went to my other best friends (who were mutual friends of my crush) and I came out. It was the first time I had ever vocalised my sexuality. It was terrifying just to say those words, even if I knew the person receiving them would be more than accepting, which they were. However, this moment was when things started to fall apart.

I found out from one of the mutual friends that the guy I had a crush on had called me 'too much'. This was a term I was all too familiar with, but hearing this term from someone I cared for so deeply hurt me to my very core. I had a falling out with him over this, which caused me a great deal of pain. My self-esteem fell off a cliff and my trust in people had completely disintegrated. This proved to be an extremely challenging period in my life. I continued with my coming out journey but the anxiety was constant. I bottled it when it came to two of my long-term best friends. We spent the whole evening together and I couldn't bring myself to say it before we parted. I ended up texting them right after, and their responses made me so happy.

I came out to another long-term best friend on our way home from, ironically, watching Moonlight at an outdoor screening. I told her just before her stop, giving her very little time to talk to me about it. Between me coming out to her and the next time we met, she had talked to her friend, who was gay, about my bisexuality and received some troubling information. Her friend had told her that bisexuality isn't really a thing and, for the most part, it is just a stepping stone to being gay.

Whilst for some people this may be the case, that doesn't mean bisexual is not a valid identity. Sexuality is a very fluid thing that can change over time. Further to this, some gay people may use bisexuality in order to 'test the waters', so to speak, if they are too scared to be entirely open about their sexuality. Whilst I am sympathetic, this only adds to the issues around bi-erasure. I had to spend the evening with my friend undoing all the misinformation she had been fed. The fact that she got this information from someone else in the LGBTQ+ community was deeply worrying and upsetting to me. It made me wonder if I would be accepted when I entered LGBTQ+ spaces. It fed into the doubts I constantly had about my sexuality and the fear I had in coming out.

I decided that I needed to come to better terms with my sexuality. I was 25 and I was still a virgin. I hadn't even kissed a person, let alone had sex with them. This always worried me and made me feel unattractive. I felt that the longer I stayed this way, the harder it would be to change it. I felt like people wouldn't want me once I told them how inexperienced I was. Even if I didn't tell them, I knew they would be able to figure it out and reject me because of it.

Being a man and a virgin made me feel like a loser, because that's how media always portrayed it. I decided to join Grindr and start exploring. This exploration really helped me get over the feeling of being unwanted. It also helped figure out the 'logistics' of having sex with another man that had always concerned me. It helped me reaffirm my sexuality and made me more comfortable with it. However, I was left with this empty feeling, this loneliness. Whilst fun, these experiences lacked the true thing that I craved, intimacy.

Eventually, I came out to my sister. As expected, she was fully supportive. But she told me there was no way I was ever going to be able to tell our parents. Whilst on the surface they appeared to be quite modern, we had come to realise their views could be very traditional. They told us that they wanted us to marry for love, not have an arranged marriage like they did, and didn't worry us with things like the caste system. However, they weren't always accepting of the partners my siblings brought home, hoping that we would all pick 'a nice

Hindu Punjabi' person. Both my mum and dad had made homophobic remarks in the past. These comments appear to come from the British Asian ideology. The strict gender roles create an imbalance between the genders and a level of toxic masculinity. Whilst this is also an issue in wider society, it feels a lot stronger within the British Asian community. This issue directly fuels the homophobic feelings that are prevalent in our community. These remarks from my parents concerned me greatly, but I knew I had to bite the bullet.

At the end of 2017, I decided to come out to my mum. She told me she wasn't happy about it, but she didn't hate me. This was probably the best outcome I could have hoped for, as I knew I wouldn't be able to get anything better than that. However, her initial remarks upset me. She stated that, 'Your dad always used to tell me not to let you play with plushes,' and then asked whether this meant I was going to start dressing like a girl. It showed just how ingrained the stereotypes of being gay are. She also tried to brush away the idea of bisexuality, saying that it's okay since I could just marry a woman. Of course I could, but it entirely depends on who I fall in love with, which I can't force or control, and marriage doesn't change my sexuality.

I never got to tell my dad nor my brother. A week or so after telling my mum, she told me that my dad already knew and had found out from my Twitter, which I was using as my safe space. I hadn't actually been speaking to my dad due to the fact that he made a joke about gay bashing, which deeply upset me. Now, all I could think about is whether he knew about my sexuality when he made this joke. I asked my mum how he felt, and the only thing she told me was that he was concerned the rest of his family would find out. This clearly meant that he was not okay with it. A few months later, I found out that the only reason he was on my Twitter was because his family had told him about it.

An argument ensued over this. Despite the way his family had acted, my dad refused to cut any ties with them. This is a common theme within Indian families. No matter how toxic your family may be, they're still family and you only get one of them. You have to constantly keep up appearances and pretend to get along, despite everything they may have said or done. It's something that I refuse to do, and I cut any remaining ties I had to my dad's family. My brother found out during this argument. Despite our rocky relationship, he sent me a wonderful message of support, which was lovely to hear.

During all of this, I was lucky to have the support of the London Gaymers. I stumbled onto this group at the end of 2017, before coming out to my mum. I was looking to get involved in the LGBTQ+ community, but had no way of doing so. I had very few LGBTQ+ friends to help me and was anxious about getting involved, as I feared I would be rejected. London Gaymers was hugely important here, as it helped bridge a gap. Video games are my main hobby, so I felt more comfortable entering this space knowing I already held a shared interest. I have made a lot of friends with people in this group, but even here bi-erasure became apparent.

During one of their events, I was talking to another bisexual guy about his experiences. He told me that he feels like a 'bad bi' because his sexual experiences are heavily skewed towards men. I responded with the fact that I had yet to do anything more than kiss a woman and that all forms of bisexuality are valid. However, a gay man overhearing our conversation then asked me how I knew I was bisexual if I had never slept with a woman. My bisexual friends and I had to then defend sexuality as removed from a person's sexual experiences. Who you have had sex with, or relationships with, does not define your sexuality – it is your thoughts and desires that do.

I marched with London Gaymers at Pride and used this to come out on Facebook. For me, this felt like the last band-aid being ripped off. I had finally come out publicly and it felt like a huge weight had been lifted off my shoulders. I could now be free to say whatever I wanted to my friends without the fear of having to come out all over again. I received a huge wealth of support from everyone on Facebook, including my mum's family.

However, the support from my mum's family was short-lived. At a family gathering my cousin, who was extremely supportive of my Facebook post, tried to erase my bisexuality. She stated I was gay and when I corrected her, she said that I probably leaned more towards guys. I had to explain to her that it's more complicated than that. Worse than this, during a discussion about my relationship with my dad, she said to me that 'No one wants their son to be gay,' and, whilst holding her one-year-old son, that she wouldn't like it if he turned out to be gay, but would accept it. The family gathering had exhausted me so much by this point that I'm ashamed to say I didn't call her out on her homophobia. On the inside, I was crying. I didn't want her son to potentially go through what I did. It was disappointing. Hearing this from my mum, an older generation, seems more understandable. Hearing this from someone who is not much older than you is so much worse. It shows just how regressive the views on homosexuality still are in my culture.

Being out in my culture is the hardest thing for me to deal with, but I'm doing it. And it feels so good to be free.

EROTIC COMPUTER

Janelle Monáe's black queer femme representation through the lens of Audre Lorde's writing

by Jessica Brough

A FEW WEEKS ago, I had the opposite of an out of body experience. I felt myself so overwhelmed I could barely speak, but my senses were heightened, my body ready to carry me through the night. My existence in that space was concrete and unapologetic.

'I've never felt more seen at a concert,' testified one of the friends I went with to see Janelle Monáe live in Manchester. As a group of Black queer womxn and non-binary people, we could all understand what they had meant. For every time Monáe sung about empowerment, moved in her Black skin with her all-Black femme dancers and all-Black band, and used her literal platform to proclaim her Pride, we felt validated, connected and loved.

Black queer femme representation is so important because it's hard to be what you can't see, and it can be hard to be proud of something so rarely celebrated in the mainstream. When societies are still claiming we do not exist or are refusing our right to exist, while they deny the truth and beauty of our identities and romantic lives, we need people like Janelle Monáe who stand up to be seen.

After the concert, I told my friend I had never been to a gig where I had been emotionally wrecked, starstruck and aroused all at the same time. Every song, every costume and blindingly white smile, every time my body made contact with the bodies of my friends beside and behind me, I felt electrified. Even now, I regularly think about that performance; an unambiguous celebration of sexuality, Blackness and womxnhood from the defiant testimony 'Django Jane' to the tender, loving song 'Pynk'. While building up to 'Make Me Feel' (her first single from LP Dirty Computer), Monáe gave us smoke-covered, silhouetted, finger clicking foreplay, with the longest intro of pose striking and moonwalking my heart and reproductive system could handle. It lasted three whole minutes.

The first time I recall seeing a similar display of sexual Black queer visibility was when I found Audre Lorde and her collection of written work in Sister Outsider. Here was a Black Lesbian Feminist so unashamed of her identity's multitudes and so readily owning her instinctive sexuality. When I got back to Edinburgh from Manchester, I immediately went back to one particular essay by Lorde, titled 'Uses of the Erotic'; a call-to-arms for women of all sexualities to see the power, creativity and politics in their erotic selves. It helped to validate my profound enjoyment of the performance and appreciate Dirty Computer specifically as an example of work from an artist who embodies Lorde's words. She writes:

'When I speak of the erotic, then, I speak of it as an assertion of the lifeforce of women; of that creative energy empowered, the knowledge and use of which we are now reclaiming in our language, our history, our dancing, our loving, our work, our lives.'[1]

When Lorde writes about power in the essay, she is talking about a charge or electrocution that you allow to pass through your whole body and into everything you do and are. When she writes about the uses of the erotic, it is an appeal to women to harness this power and to let it light up your life, give it meaning, without shame or societal baggage. Lorde's essay provides a lens through which to appreciate Janelle Monáe; positioning herself and others as 'Dirty Computers' is to embrace uniqueness without sanitising or censoring to appease oppressors.

We can use the same lens to validate the thrill we receive from art that moves us and shocks our systems. When we find the content that hits us in that way, we would do well to take Lorde's advice and fall freely into the erotic feeling of it – 'an internal sense of satisfaction to which, once we have experienced it, we know we can aspire'. With this, she is reminding us not to settle – find the things that get you going and get going with them. For me, this has involved exploring and revelling in my Blackness, queerness and gender expression in all their distinct and tangled ways.

At the tail end of the same month I saw Janelle Monáe live, I took myself to see Joan Armatrading at Usher Hall. Here was an iconic dark-skinned lesbian singing love songs about women in one of Edinburgh's most famous venues. That night I embraced the erotic when I dressed up for myself, cupped my red wine and cried during one of my all-time favourite pseudo-love songs 'Love and Affection', flanked either side by similarly emotional lesbian couples twice my age.

Black queer music is the gift that challenges and inspires. When I watched the music video for 'Make Me Feel' for the first time, I wasn't expecting to be left feeling so flustered and ultimately so turned on – it was a revelation that any music video could have such an effect on me.

Over a year later, I'm sitting here blushing as I watch it again for the nth time. Its undeniable queerness includes Monáe running between a leather jacketed handsome man and sky-high stilettoed actress Tessa Thompson during what could be described as a physical representation of the Kinsey Scale. Accompanied by Prince-inspired guitar licks and shuddering synthesisers, we really didn't stand a chance getting through this track alive. So when Janelle Monáe starts singing? About sex and attraction? In that voice? Well, it's *so good so good so fucking real*.

In her essay, Lorde talks about the fear and shame in the erotic. So badly understood, the erotic has been given a deliberately unfair reputation of sleaze and privacy; something you experience behind closed doors with maybe one other person. She argues the erotic has been packaged in this way to control women, because allowing it to flourish would threaten the carefully constructed systems of societal oppression. Instead, we should strive to appreciate both the individual and collective joy in the erotic and recognise that 'women so empowered are dangerous', full of agency to change our world. I compare my experience of willingly crying alone at Usher Hall to the group that naturally formed around my friends and me of Black femmes at Monáe's concert, all of us experiencing the erotic together. In both instances I felt seen in the absence of fear or shame – understood within Armatrading's lyrics, and sharing my deepest joy with a group watching Monáe perform to us. These are energised feelings that can spark revolutions.

Admitting I found Monáe's performance arousing was not embarrassing, and absolutely living for a song or a performance is never shameful. To let yourself be completely and utterly taken over by someone else's creativity, turning it into yourself and finding it existing in a place deep inside of you where it feels phenomenal, is exactly what Lorde was preaching.

'In the way my body stretches to music and opens into response, hearkening to its deepest rhythms, so every level upon which I sense also opens to the erotically satisfying experience, whether it is dancing, building a bookcase, writing a poem, examining an idea.'

Since coming out publicly as queer, Janelle Monáe's status as Black queer icon has skyrocketed. But let's not get this twisted – despite only recently feeling ready to be so publicly candid about how she loves, Monáe has been singing about sexuality and producing queer content for years. On her debut LP The ArchAndroid, she sings teasingly about the mutual attraction and affection for the rosy cheeked Blueberry Mary on 'Mushrooms & Roses' (it's not subtle). Watch out for the moment she sings the line 'kissing friends' then winks at the camera in the femme-centric video for 'Dance Apocalyptic'. Back in 2010 she performed 'Tightrope' on Jools Holland in her then-classic uniform of a crisp white dinner shirt, black bow tie and afro quiff. I was working in a suit shop in 2010 and remember looking at the men's formal wear in envy – I recall this performance as one of many chapters in my queer awakening.

In 2013, Monáe released the album The Electric Lady and, with it, the exploding funk sensation 'Q.U.E.E.N'. Did you catch the moment she actually gasps the word 'queer' in the backing vocals of the first chorus? As well as being an incredible song to dance to and a guaranteed spirit soaring ride, the track is a straight-up Pride anthem. Overall the lyrics are empowering, unapologetic and forthright, but the third verse hints at the uncertainty that can accompany queerness and acceptance. When you do not fit a heteronormative mould and embracing your desires might get you labelled a 'freak', is it better to just 're-programme de-programme and get down'?

We are reminded that the search for approval or being 'good enough' is never more important that your authenticity. By the end of the song, it is clear Monáe has no intention of changing to suit society's conditions, but every intention of changing those conditions. According to the now legendary interview with Rolling Stone magazine, Monáe originally called the song 'Q.U.E.E.R'[2]. While that title would have been ground-breaking five years ago, it is a lesson that it's okay to change something as small as a letter till we are ready to share a big truth with the world.

In the same interview, Monáe labels herself as a 'Free-Ass Motherfucker' – when she uses this descriptor, we get the sense she's telling us who she is, without feeling required to explain it every single time. Free-Ass Motherfuckers leave room for growth and change, and reject expectations and standards of the dominating rule-makers of society. They embody what Audre Lorde was talking about in 'Uses of the Erotic'.

> 'Our erotic knowledge empowers us, becomes a lens through which we scrutinize all aspects of our existence, forcing us to evaluate those aspects honestly in terms of their relative meaning within our lives. And this is a grave responsibility, projected from within each of us, not to settle for the convenient, the shoddy, the conventionally expected, nor the merely safe.'

With her genre-bending, androgynous styling and fierce support for her community, Janelle Monáe has never been 'safe'. Her visibility and art will continue to give power to the Black queer femmes who were born hard-wired for the erotic current of rule-defying pop, ready for it to pass through their dirty mainframes.

ALL THE THINGS SHE SAID

by Annie Dobson

1. SHE SAID,
'And since when were you into girls?'
and pushed her against the wall, stuck her hand down her pants.

I am 15 and watching the first episode of Lip Service, a sort of Scottish version of The L Word, on the tiny, five-channel telly in my bedroom, volume on three, baby-finger on the off button. Sex Education never told us about butches, about femmes, about how to exist outside of a pornographic category.

I want to live in the Glasgow-utopia of Lip Service. I don't know the word utopia yet. It will be eight years until I write an essay on queer heterotopias. I don't know the word queer. I don't know the word bisexual. I know lesbian. I know lesbian is pornographic is Other is secret. I know I am a secret. I know how to delete my search history. I don't know anything about queer history. I can't remember if there were bisexual characters in Lip Service, probably not, but at that age, it was enough.

Earlier that evening, I would have played *The Sims* because I played *The Sims* every day. I did not know I was playing in a *queer utopia*: Sims can interact with other Sims romantically/sexually regardless of gender. To put it in a way I like: *all Sims are bisexual*. *The Sims* came out in 2000 and same-sex marriage has always been a feature. *The Sims* was fourteen years ahead of the UK government.

I suck myself into screens: technology has always saved me this way.

2. She said,
'Lezzbian Sexxx Stories :P Read Hereee XP'
and I clicked on it. 12 years old, I was on Stardoll.com, a dress-up doll site. I was *Candydreamer* and here is where I learnt about Alexander McQueen and badly written lesbian erotica. Sex is everywhere and the internet in 2007 was no less bizarre.

There would be dolls with usernames like p-u-s-x-x-y-l-u-v-a, like lizzzz-bian. They would write their fantasies on their pages, in the albums used to document outfits and write little descriptions. In retrospect, I wonder how old these people truly were. And, though I don't want to think this, I don't want to think of this at all – I always wonder if these people were men.

The internet has always scared me this way.

3. She said,
'I think she fancies you.'
and I am sixteen and nervous, laughing and trying so hard not to be *found out*. She was outcasted, she was a *weird fucking lesbian*. We talked about Sylvia Plath and she introduced me to Tumblr, to riot grrrl. In retrospect, she was the coolest girl in our school. We went to school in working-class West Yorkshire, on the border of Leeds and Wakefield, between

nothing and nothing and no *wokeness*, so uncool to be liberal in any way (except, thankfully, you couldn't be a Tory), a school of *make me a sammich*, of *I'm not racist but*.

Let me walk you around my high school for a day and then take you back in the time machine to 2015 when I go on Tinder for the first time in my hometown on the Easter holidays. Look at all the girls here, lesbian/bisexual girls who once sat and laughed when the other girls, not seeing them as *other girls*, talked about their future daughters and how disgusted they would be if those imaginary daughters loved other imaginary daughters.

And again and again, I suck myself into screens: technology has always saved me this way. Technology has always hurt me like:

That evening, she was in a Facebook official relationship with a boy. It was the first time my stomach would *do the drop*. The next day, sitting next to her in English, she kept saying *my boyfriend, my boyfriend*. I realised I Liked her with a capital L, *like as in like like*, I liked her like I had liked boys. I liked her more than I had liked boys. I absolutely hated her. I absolutely hated that there was a possibility of someone like me, someone at a school like our school, and then suddenly there wasn't. At this point, I never considered that she was hiding herself, or that maybe she was bisexual, that maybe she was possibly even more *like me* than I had thought.

4. She said,
'Stop crying about boys and date a girl.'

I am at *art school*, which is really humanities school, which is really Goldsmiths, University of London, known for its *wokeness*, its liberalness, so unlike my high school, everyone so unlike everyone at my high school, the closest thing to the Glasgow-utopia of *Lip Service*, where queer is fine, queer is quotidian. Most of my close friends are bisexual girls. It is so freeing to talk about any gender, for everyone to have their Tinder settings on *Women and Men*, to put on 'All the Things She Said' at pre-drinks and laugh about ourselves as scared little baby-queers. This open life, 200 miles away from Yorkshire, is what I always wanted but again, she says,

'Boys are trash. Date a girl.'

and she's right, but I can't take her advice. I keep falling in love (read: *I keep experiencing idealisation because of my borderline personality disorder*) with boys. Pining over a boy is *anti-feminist*, is *so fucking het*, is *not very radical, is it?*

So uncool.

I don't feel very radical. I read Dworkin and hate men. I hate my attraction to men, my attraction to men feels *anti-feminist*. I read about political lesbians on Tumblr, I read about how much *real* lesbians hate them. The personal is political but I don't want my partner to be an accessory to my righteousness. I don't want to date anyone where their gender is my primary reason for dating them. I love (a lot of, but not all of) Dworkin, but I read Roxane Gay's *Bad Feminist* and feel better. I consider my privilege of being able to date whoever I want regardless of gender and feel better. I consider my sexuality as still-radical anyway, still a fuck-you to heteronormativity and feel better.

5. She said,

'Do you know what borderline personality disorder is?'

and I am diagnosed, I am legally-medically-officially *emotionally unstable* (lol) and one of the nine symptoms is *promiscuity*, filed under impulsivity and a *need for validation*, a *need for attention*. One of the biggest bisexual stereotypes is that we are *promiscuous*, that we are attention seekers. On one particularly self-loathing night, I read an article on *The Daily Beast* called 'Borderline Personality Disorder and Sex'. It begins with, 'To some men, women with *Borderline Personality*

Disorder hold an irresistible allure in bed. Gina Piccalo on the mental illness that can lead to wild sex.' I feel sick, I feel pornographic, I feel fetish, I feel dragged back to 15, to 12.

The internet always hurts me like this.

The male fantasy of the bisexual woman looks like the sister of the fantasy borderline. Sisters, not siblings, because both are female-coded, though in truth, of course, any gender can be either/both.

Sexual attraction to more than one gender, to some psychiatrists, can be read as *sexual impulsivity*, a *wildness*. I don't think there is anything inherently wrong in being *promiscuous*. There is a difference between promiscuity and sex as self-harm. There is *agency* and there is being taken advantage of. And anyway, who decides what is promiscuous? How many sexual partners is that? How many genders? The idea of promiscuity, in itself, is either female-coded or used to refer to gay/bisexual men. The only one of us who is not morally damned is the heterosexual man.

Sexual attraction to more than one gender, to some psychiatrists, can be seen as part of an *unstable sense of self*, an *identity disturbance*. But switching from dating a boy to dating a girl isn't the same as cutting all my hair off and announcing I am going to be a seamstress (who has never picked up a needle and thread). When I date a girl, I don't announce myself as a lesbian; when I date a boy, I don't announce myself as straight.

(Bisexual and borderline, the double Bs, rereading the nine criteria on the bus home, my head is full of bees.)

The lesbian comedian Hannah Gadsby, in her acclaimed comedy set *Nanette*, says that intellectually she knows her sexuality is not something to be ashamed of. Intellectually, I know these Bs are not something to be ashamed of, but here I am, deleting tweets, hiding the Bs under my bed when anyone comes over. Gadsby says that intellectually she knows this, but – and she points to her heart – 'but right here, I still have shame.'

Sadly, there is a certain necessity, a certain self-protection in silence. Statistically, bisexual women are nearly twice as likely to experience domestic violence. A characterization of BPD is *a pattern of unstable and intense interpersonal relationships*. Symptoms like *fear of abandonment* and emotional sensitivity can easily lead to abuse, especially gaslighting: *I didn't do anything wrong, you're overreacting because of your BPD.* The trope of heterosexual men asking for threesomes with their bisexual partners is an eyeroll, an annoyance, but this kind of thinking, this equating bisexuality with complete sexual openness and desire to please men, possibly so they won't leave you, can be much more serious. The double Bs can be dangerous.

The DSM stopped considering homosexuality a mental illness in 1987. LGBTQ+ people experience mental health problems more than the general population. But we know this is environmental, a product of growing up Other in a heteronormative society, not some internal pathology.

Bisexuality is seen as the *borderline* between gay and straight. BPD was previously thought of as the *borderline* between psychosis and neurosis. A key feature of BPD is *black and white thinking*, everything is either/or. This either/or doesn't leave me wishing to be either gay or straight, there is no pause before ticking 'bisexual' on a medical form. But still, I lay down in this liminal space, this grey and glitchy after-hours office, and close off all my tabs of (cishet) men telling me who I am, which pornographic category to file me under.

6. She said,
'Bisexuality is a myth invented to sell flavoured vodka'
on the trailer of a new comedy, *The Bisexual*, and I scream. Another trailer comes on for the first bisexual dating show

and yes, again, I scream. I have just turned 24, it is 2018, I have lived in eight houses since the tiny bedroom telly, but I am still sucking myself into screens this way, crawling into these queer utopias. Like the bisexual stereotype, like the borderline stereotype, I will always be desperate and greedy (for Bisexual Content™).

'BISEXUAL WOMAN HAS SEX WITH GAY MAN'

Not such an unusual story

by Alizée Pichot

To THAT DAY, my sexual and romantic encounters and relation-ships had been fulfilled by both men and women – including hetero, bi and gay women as well as hetero and bi men. When I recall the positive (and some loving) duos I was part of, gender did matter to me because it helped me calibrate what sexual role I would fit myself in when the time came.

'Did I really see in terms of gender before?' This was the first question in my head right after the moment he touched me. Even the essential idea of a fixed sexuality linked (or not) to one immutable gender seemed like a huge misunderstanding, may I say, an irony.

The traditionally accepted 'once in a lifetime' connotation of the word 'experience' was being turned over and trans-formed. On the contrary, every part of me had just learnt something eternal. The kind of lesson that makes you believe you could never go back again.

Here is my first point, then: despite being criticised and diminished amongst some self-proclaimed pro-sex feminists (a group in which I include myself), heterosexuality (read: male/female sexual relationships) is not as limited as it appears. In fact (disclaimer, major announcement coming!), heterosexual activity can be très gay, too!

When I was younger, around 17–18, at the peak of my queer consciousness and self-recognition, I saw myself as the out and fierce heterosexual girl who loved to kiss other girls. In other words, it was almost impossible at the time to use the words 'lesbian' or 'gay' referring to myself because of the social stigma all around me. But the uncertainty of sexual feelings/orientation was never really a 'no-go zone' for me. I knew I wanted to explore and meet different bodies, different souls, struggling with and loving a potential future as a non-hetero woman.

I do understand people not dating folks who are not completely out of the closet because they fear they will be hurt – I do, but don't relate. The gap between two people can sometimes be huge, but history has proven humans are really good at building bridges. Facing an unsure person whilst being naked – and vulnerable – forces us to compromise, to think before touching, to ask, to express ourselves and listen to each other.

That said, as a bisexual cis woman (wanting to wear the label or not is a whole other discussion) recognising and living the inner fluidity of genders and sexualities, I was honestly caught by surprise when I was about to sexually meet a gay man.

I felt immersed in life so greatly, so earthily, as if I had finally realised all those words I read and wrote and listened to. The word 'experience' took on a whole new meaning, so much more accurate to my current life-spinning moment. I felt deeply under my skin the importance of the experience that had just happened.

Having real, kind-hearted sex with a man who loves men was like everything I hadn't known before. Nothing with him was taken for granted. From either side. Neither of us knew our connection would blossom that way, so joyfully, so vividly. And thus, none of the steps we stood upon was taken for granted. Of course, at the beginning, I had assumed as fact that he wouldn't be attracted or interested in me, and I wasn't naturally inclined to think of him in that way either. Et pourtant...

The first smile, the first confession, the first giggle, the first acceptance, the first touch, the first kiss, whisper, warm breath on my neck, hand on my breast, my hips, my ass, my...

'Fuck, we're naked! It's happening.' I'm pretty sure we both heard this thought fly through each other's minds, spinning.

His cis-male body was familiar to me, as I have sex with cis men regularly. Still, he was unique and one of a kind in reactions and sensibility, but still familiar and non-threatening. The biggest difference I could notice at the time that separated this encounter from other 'purely' heterosexual ones was the uniqueness of the touch, of the glance we let wander over each other. Everything felt like a first time infused with euphoria, doubtless joy and discovery.

He had not touched a woman for several years, and I am a woman of sensuality; the smallest touch can be overwhelmingly good, which frightened him a bit at first. I understood and we talked for a while, cuddling and smiling about all the good things about to happen. Everything around us seemed to exhale magic, a perfect sentiment d'immatérialité (maybe the quality weed helped a bit).

During this night, I approached areas of male (or not – what do I know?) sexuality that I had never explored. Here I was, with a naked god on my bed, him breathless and I full of sensations and shivers travelling my own body, negotiating pleasure at every turn.

I bet you're dying to read the dirty little details. This moment was too precious for me to tell the whole magic, but

I will unveil one truth we discovered, one that needs to be anchored in both our sexual pasts and preferences, though I can only tell my story here.

All right, let's do this. By having sex with both men and women, I learnt that I am what we could call versatile (my gay male friends taught me this word). It means that the way I offer myself or participate in the sexual relationship can vary; I can love to be willingly submissive with men as much as I like to stay fully clothed to give a woman pleasure and dominate her in a gentle way (or less gentle, depending). Before him, I already knew I could extend the spectrum of my sexual preferences even more, but had never gotten the chance to actually do it.

With this amazing person, and thanks to both our mutual experiences and knowledge of our own likings, we went past our comfort zones. I accepted the desire to control a man's body through pleasure, to penetrate him in ways that I'd never known, and he naturally let me do it, asking me to envelop him with my instinct to give and receive in other ways.

Both our natural habits of pleasure were satisfied. I did not want to be penetrated by a penis and he did not want to be inside a vagina. He knew how to give a hole a lot of love and I know how to suck dick. What a perfect combination – wait, surprise! – not centred around ejaculation or systematic orgasm. It was simple and natural and required a lot of talking, checking if everything was okay. We were *en phase*.

Maybe because it was everything but expected, the intensity and greatness of the moment overwhelmed both of us; it was like we had discovered a secret about humanity, touched one of the most hypocritical aspects of a society which puts people – and teaches us to put ourselves – in non-communicative boxes of sexuality and genders. We had to do it fully to know, to be sure, to be able to say, 'It is possible to go past these norms, we actually did it!'

Afterward, my world was shaken upside down. I couldn't help but project the film of this night over and over in my head. I was afraid to fall in love again, to be intoxicated by the awesome amount of desire that had overcome me. The strength of desire and attraction to another unknown human made me forget all the one-night stands I had had before. Time went by, feelings blurred and now I keep this night warm in my heart; surely it will be cherished till the end of times (or just my life, really).

The weight of this everlasting experience is yet to be fixed; I have no idea if such an encounter will happen again. In the same sense, I am not sure exactly how my one-night partner felt in the week following us touching. What I know is that it created a very special bond between us. The way we look and talk to each other now is full of tenderness, a silent understanding that something else is possible.

Sex can be such a caress to the soul, a lifetime opening for human knowledge, a soft breach of light coming into the heart and a sweet fire to the body. No matter who you have sex with, it is important not to forget why you do it, what makes you want to throw your clothes away and devour someone else's skin with kisses. Try to understand the origins of the butterflies in your stomach and stick to them! Don't let fear or norms get in the way of your sensual universe; it is way bigger than you. Let the flow get to you, enter the party where surrounding energies will guide you to special people, show you the path of liberty and self-empowerment.

I now have the certainty to be able to travel in my own skin, even though it doesn't fit into society's standards. I don't care anymore, I will let myself be attracted to anyone who deserves it and shows respect to my life as a human.

I swear that I will not try to define someone else's sexual orientation or gender just to reassure myself. I swear to love and encourage consensual sex with whomever wishes to speak of it with me, because it is such a great part of life, of a very real and feeling-oriented passage *sur la terre*.

THANK GOD FOR STRAIGHT CIS MALE ARTISTS!

by Chay Collins

I MEAN THIS title completely sincerely. I used to be a straight cis man in a little bubble. I come from a small village, so sometimes my only escape was cinema. This isn't a story about seeing myself reflected on screen, but rather the screen inviting me to question myself. When you're a kid you don't question mainstream media – which is dominated by white, straight, able-bodied cis men. But once you start exploring, you do sometimes see the mainstream push at the fringes.

One person who did this is Jim Carrey. He is an amazing actor; his gangly ability to morph into a role is spectacularly impressive. When I was young, I first saw him in roles such as The Mask and Ace Ventura, but his versatility is what drew me to explore his entire filmography; particularly his serious roles, e.g. The Truman Show or The Number 23. At some point it was inevitable I would see I Love You Phillip Morris.

I Love You Phillip Morris is arguably one of the best Hollywood representations of gay men because it subverts so many mainstream tropes: sex scenes, the AIDS crisis and the homosexual as a criminal, etc. Jim Carrey brings his usual rubbery energy, but instils sombre and tender emotions into the romance with Ewan McGregor. For my film course, I wrote an essay about how this fit into homo pomo cinema, a term coined by B Ruby Rich (before New Queer Cinema) that categorises queer cinema through its irreverent energy and its joyous embrace of rejecting positive imagery and taking deviant pleasure in queer characters being flawed and committing crime. For example, Steven Russell, Jim Carrey's character in *I Love You Phillip Morris*, is motivated to try to find his true self by conning people into letting him play out different professional and social positions. The sex he has is portrayed as fun and he celebrates his identity as a gay man. But it is through his unrelenting love for his partner Phillip Morris that he is able to find his place within the world. In the course of my research my eyes were opened to the breadth of queer cinema at large.

I remember teasing a boy on a bus home from college for giving another man a blowjob. No one deserves to be bullied to any degree, but I played along with the teasing because I was ashamed of something within myself. No one ever told me explicitly that being gay was wrong, but everyone who is a part of the supposed norm without thinking about it believes everyone outside it is up for ridicule – or, in other cases, worse.

I didn't think being gay was morally wrong, but I thought the act of physically doing anything sexual with a man was gross. I had feelings for men but I repressed them. It's very easy to dismiss them when you also have feelings for women, and it would take a while longer to come more to terms with this. But *I Love You Phillip Morris* showed me how homosexuality is positive and normal and that as a person it is okay to try out different versions of yourself. That's because of Jim Carrey, who found it acceptable to play a gay character and even relished it.

I was obsessed with actors – like Carrey – and by chance I saw an advert for a film playing on Film4 late at night about entering the mind of an actor. The film was *Being John Malkovich* and I was compelled to stay up and watch it. I loved it. It encouraged me to pursue my interest in cinema and showed me that films weren't just vehicles for actors; films were ways for writers, directors and a whole crew to tell stories.

Unfortunately, the film also imprinted on me in another way. As a young confused teenage boy, I identified with the sadness and unreciprocated love experienced by the protagonist Craig Schwartz. It's funny to me now that he's the one I identified with, as he's clearly not the hero of the story, committing abhorrent actions due to his fragile masculinity. I unfortunately kept Craig intertwined with my own identity for a while, but I also kept Charlie Kaufman, the screenwriter, with me too.

When Kaufman directed his first film *Synecdoche, New York*, I couldn't wait to see it, and when I finally did I hated it. But it was one of those films that niggled away at me. Eventually I watched it a second time and I saw that I hated it because of how it affected me in a deeply scary way – the film is a masterpiece and endlessly re-watchable. Though I didn't know why at the time, my mind locked into the theme of gender and led me to write a dissertation on masculinity as a self-imposed simulacrum and the repression of the transgenderism of Caden Cotard, the protagonist. Exploring ideas surrounding gender led to an exploration of my own gender; first trying out cross-dressing, then feeling very much like I wasn't a man, identifying as non-binary and, well, I don't think I have finished the trajectory of this exploration. Seeing Caden waste their life and not have it fulfilled by exploring themself as a woman and expressing their potential sexual attraction to men was a horror. I did not want to end up like Caden, whose own narcissistic self-obsession with the perception of themself stifled their growth.

By inspiring me to explore my own and Caden's genders through reading academic theory, Kaufman had also brought me to feminism. Once a young teenager who called a woman 'it' on social media, I'm now able to have deeper intimate connections and respect for women and to see why both Craig in *Being John Malkovich* and I were assholes.

Speaking of assholes, in polite society they are deemed disgusting. One function is kept in our minds so that we won't think of that area as sexual. This repressed my self-exploration and I thought that I wouldn't be into having anything inside me, but then I listened to *Harmontown*.

Watching *Community*, an American sitcom that shows a group of people from different backgrounds and viewpoints come together to define their own truths, I wanted to hear more from the voice of its creator, Dan Harmon. I would listen to *Harmontown* all the time; at my job as a labourer, on countryside walks, alone in my room. After moving back home from university, I had to find something that filled the time of village life again. I found the people on *Harmontown* sincere as they stumbled, unedited, through their problematic behaviours.

And so, in one of Harmon's many moments of openly expressing anything and everything he's ever done, he told a story about sticking a Sharpie pen up his butt while masturbating. He explained why he didn't enjoy it, but expressed how he never wanted to regret not trying it. As a fan of Dan Harmon I wanted to emulate him, changing my viewpoint to not wanting to regret. Looking for the thinnest thing nearby, something I was sure wouldn't get lost, I stuck a HB pencil – eraser end first – inside of me. This moment was not that pleasant (or safe), but it was certainly interesting enough to explore further. In the future, it would lead to some of the most pleasurable times in my life.

Sticking something up an asshole is no more disgusting than sticking something up anywhere else, or putting your mouths or hands places. It was a taboo that Dan Harmon helped me break.

I say thank you to these straight men so much because without them I wouldn't have found myself.

That said, queer casting is an issue that is regularly debated. I strongly stand for a gender-specific character to be played by someone of that gender. Or if the character is trans, to cast the role with someone who can imbue it with the correct truth. For example, in the film They, the character J is assigned male at birth and unsure about their next step in transition. However, the actor who portrays them, Rhys Fehrenbacher, is a trans man. Even if a cis actor can perform the role well and actually provide a brilliant representation – for example, Toma Ikuta in Close-Knit – the wonderful Jen Richards lays out why cis people shouldn't play trans roles in her video response on the casting of the film Anything. The main reason being that the idea a trans woman is just a man in drag leads to violence in real life, against trans women specifically. Fragile straight cis dudes dating trans women lash out in violence to assert masculinity when people say that they're gay.

But I am still torn on whether heterosexuals can play a character of a different sexuality. In some of my favourite examples, shows like Sense8 and Please Like Me, they have straight actors playing gay characters, but they also have queer actors represented and queer authorial voices behind shaping the stories and imagery with authenticity*. The other issue is

---

* Just because these shows and others have queer authorial voices does not mean they

that casting directors are not meant to ask actors their sexuality, a policy meant to protect queer actors but which instead often hinders them. A lot of actors sometimes feel they can't come out for fear that audiences may not believe them in a romantic film between a man and a woman. Straight actors do not get discriminated against for what roles they audition for and play whilst LGBTQ+ actors still do. So although some queer actors feel they are getting typecast, some feel they do not even get roles. Therefore, a straight actor cast in a non-heterosexual role is taking away a job and continues to keep doors shut to the queer community.

I still think I *Love You Phillip Morris* is one of the best American movies in queer cinema, but so is *The Watermelon Woman* by Cheryl Dunye, which has queer actors in queer roles. I totally accept Jim Carrey in *I Love You Phillip Morris* because it is clearly not a film made to garner him accolades, but is instead grounded in the unfathomable true life of Steven Russell, who lives his life without regret. He is out and unabashedly so. There are issues with queer casting, but if it weren't for Jim Carrey, a straight actor in a gay role, I wouldn't have found myself and been further opened up to queer cinema with queer actors.

Although I'm not sure what Charlie Kaufman's sexual orientation is, I was definitely drawn to his straight male characters. But it was my deeper dive into exploring and reading cinema that revealed different communities, perspectives and life questions, and Kaufman started me on that path. When I watch films now, I can't help but see feminist and gender issues in them. I'll watch *Girlhood* or *Moonlight* and see the issues of gender performance within them. Through

---

are by any means perfect. Both shows coming from white creators has led to problematic racial representation in both shows and there are arguments for certain moments being problematic in its queer representation.

his characters, Charlie Kaufman showed what it is like to live with the regret of not exploring ourselves, and instead keeping ourselves locked in a system that would destroy us. I wouldn't have explored myself and questioned systems if it weren't for Charlie Kaufman.

And Dan Harmon told me to explore my body because I shouldn't regret it even if I didn't like it (I did like it). But more than this, Harmon told me to go out and make mistakes, to know when you make mistakes, to listen to others, to better yourself. It may have been the best thing I've ever done with a pencil, and I'm a writer.

A lot of people have a story about seeing themselves reflected on screen and then coming to terms with it. Although I see myself in queer characters now, I wouldn't have been able to back then. Instead, it was straight voices exploring queer aspects that opened the door for me. Their art was able to turn me from a straight male, with actions and thoughts I now regret, to the proud non-binary bisexual I am today.

We need more LGBTQIA+ voices and voices from other marginalised communities in our media, and more exposure to them in our youth. We need our identities presented as a normality. But for me, if it weren't for those, straight and cis men exploring these stories, I would never have found queer media.

ZUGEHÖRIGKEIT

Where do I belong?

by T. Ludwig

IT WAS ON a Tuesday night in a random Berlin bar. My fellow student Miriam opened her eyes in disbelief. '*Are you also into guys?*' I nodded with a sheepish grin and my inner monitor changed the pilot light to 'drunk'. Otherwise I would not have had the courage to tell her.

So this was what my coming out as bisexual felt like. And it felt good. I never thought my sexual identity was something I was supposed to pin on my jacket. I wished I could be that open.

But with a conservative background and some – *really bad* – experiences, I had a way of not letting this question come up (which is kind of difficult in a language like mine – German – where almost everything is marked with a grammatical gender). I always felt a little odd when it came to sexuality and telling my story. Most of the times when my sexual orientation became an issue, it felt like opening Pandora's box over and over again.

This time, with this specific circle of friends, I never found it important to tell them. They knew about my long-term relationship, which was something I always wanted. And no further questions were asked. This felt good. After years of struggling, of not belonging to any group, of people questioning my choice of partners – this was a place where no one cared, no one judged.

My first years at school I got singled out – or I singled myself out – from the group of boys that always wanted to play soccer, talked about cars and other things that I regarded as boyish nonsense. Later I grew fond of literature, art and fashion and talked a lot about philosophical and religious questions. I did not mind, because I had a good circle of friends back then.

The first group that definitively felt uncomfortable with me was the religious group I grew up in. Well, to be honest, it was me who wasn't completely at ease while listening to them, such as when they were talking about 'the gays'. They sometimes said that the gays were people to be loved, but the rest of the conversation surely did not sound like they meant it seriously.

Growing up and going through puberty I fell in and out of love, and had my crushes. The crushes I had on girls were no problem; after all, it was something that – according to the script – was supposed to happen. There were certain rules when it came to dating and you had to follow a certain protocol. But this was not an issue for me. What really made me worry was that I also felt this weird attraction to guys. I could not put my finger on it – and so began my quest for a role model.

On different occasions I felt like I was not able to bear the internal struggle by myself anymore and I turned to people in my social group for help. I had a couple of friends that handled it rather well in spite of their apparent confusion.

Others turned to the sole objective of praying the gay away. Somehow I was convinced all my feelings had to be something temporary. But they weren't.

Was I really gay? What about the feelings I had for girls too? I struggled with myself, with my feelings for guys and the question of how my faith was part of all this. I decided not to talk to anyone about that. I hoped on the one hand I could be heterosexual, to fit in. But at the same time I wanted a definite proof that I was gay. The only way of getting this that came to mind was to just try it. I had not had a sexual encounter until my early twenties.

At university I got to know a guy and we got into talking a lot about different things. In German you say you talk about god and the world – 'über Gott und die Welt,' which means just about everything that comes into your mind. He was really charming and very interested in my views and as it went, we also came upon sexuality. One of the following weeks after he started to talk to me, he asked me over to his place. It would be a relaxed and fun night, he promised.

It turned into a threesome – which I never asked for. His friend dropped me at home late that night and I fell into a short and restless sleep. I woke up early the next morning and felt like I had been hit by a train. I could not measure the shame and the angst that got into me. My gay test proved positive. What did that mean? I did not know where to turn. I knew my family and the religious people in my social circle would most certainly condemn me. So I called up last-night's-guy and asked him what exactly the night had meant to him. I asked if he thought I was gay, since I experienced some pleasant moments. He was not in the mood to talk to me: 'Don't you worry. You are not gay. You just had a little fun. Let's do it another time.' And he disconnected the line. At that moment my world fell apart. I fell into an abyss. The next couple of weeks I wandered the streets of the town late at night and cried myself to sleep.

My thoughts seemed like a merry-go-round that spun out of control. The next months I did not dare to speak to anyone about this. I hated myself for my feelings. I could not place things in order. I wanted someone to talk me through it. Questions about faith and sexuality turned into a blur. I got quieter and lonelier since I was sure no one would want to listen to my view of the story. Religious people would tell me to stop thinking such nonsense and get a grip, while non-religious people would disdain me for even bothering to ask such questions. They would tell me to just live my life and not allow myself to be chained in. I knew I belonged to both groups but at the same time, I felt both groups would not accept me until I renounced the other and just focused on their cause. But it was not a cause, it was not a matter of choice. It was my life that was at stake.

I started reading all kinds of stuff. I delved into classic literature, religious handbooks and into the internet in my search for redemption. After I felt like I had read through all the theory without getting even close to something that gave me any relief, I decided it was time for action. I started being active on all the apps and went into a phase of intensive dating. Maybe that was the way for me to find a person that really accepted me. If not, at least I would get physical affection.

Some of the relationships I pursued were of an abusive nature, which I only realised later. From my current perspective I believe the late realisation was for the best. I do not know if I could have handled both the internal struggle and the weight of voluntarily putting myself into this kind of relationship where people couldn't care less about my physical integrity.

At this point, I was almost sure I was just gay. I still

managed to keep the dating hidden from family, friends and people who knew me from classes. Meanwhile, I kept going to religious meetings and started to ask questions about 'the gays'. I wanted to get my religious peers thinking. But I did not reveal myself. In between my dates, I still sometimes longed for a female presence in my life.

Later that year, I had a crush on an Italian exchange student who was openly gay and I decided to befriend him. He seemed to be a person who cared about others and had a variety of interests that I genuinely shared. I have no explicit memory of making the decision to put all my energy into getting him to notice me. Maybe I just went with my gut feeling. It was a good decision. We started conversations about culture and literature. I told him that one of the books I was reading was *Separate Rooms* by the Italian writer Tondelli, which almost made me cry in the library. He knew a little bit about the author and was surprised that I would know his writings.

As I came out to him and confessed my attraction to him he handled it very well. This was the acceptance I was missing. I was so surprised that he turned me down but kept being a good friend to me that I didn't even mind the rejection. I had found something I needed way more than a relationship. He was a real friend.

He really did care about me. He talked to me about different issues, from coming out to believing in one's self-worth and showing some backbone to certain people. He made me take an HIV test and introduced me to all these places I would not have gone by myself. I started to develop a self-esteem that I never thought possible before. And I started to feel accepted as I began to make myself visible in the gay scene.

At the same time, I moved to a flat with just female students. One of them was always travelling for the first months

I lived there, so I didn't particularly notice her. Only later, she started to invite me to tag along to parties and found all kinds of reasons to hang out with me. I felt at ease and did not realise that she had a severe crush on me. She started to hang out in my room and we would talk a lot. She realised that there was something I was hiding, something I did not handle very well. Sometimes I was still haunted by living a secretive life and the possibility of me having a relationship with women.

One night we talked about how religion and the LGBTQ+ world had such high fences between them and how it had to be even harder for those who lived in between those two worlds – or on the fence. I felt this was the cue for me. I told her about the conflict in my life. And the waterworks started running. We grew closer by the day. I felt at ease in her presence because I knew that she did not judge me, but was genuinely interested in me as a person.

I did not respond to her crush on me because I was afraid of hurting her. I felt I belonged with her but it was not possible. After all, I thought I was gay.

But the friendship grew stronger and stronger. Up to the point where people were asking what exactly the reason was why we were not together. I asked that of myself too. Was it not impossible for a gay man to start a 'straight' relationship? It had to be crooked on one way or the other. I would be kidding myself. After a lot of time I finally gave in. No, not to my feelings – I did not act against my feelings, but against something most people around me believed. That there is either straight or queer. They thought it was madness to try to break out of this pattern. I should have not listened to those people – it would have spared me so much pain.

It seemed that my decision to start a relationship with a girl made some of my gay friends really insecure, or mad or worried. They came on to me to prove to me where I really belonged. They were sure that my relationship was something doomed to failure. I worried about myself, my sexuality, my integrity. I lost many friends during these months and I was glad that my studies and two jobs kept me busy and left little time for conversations. Once again, I seemed to have left a group that claimed absolute loyalty to their principles.

Some of my religious friends came to me and had the 'I told you so – you would end up with a girl, you are normal' talk. I was furious – did they know about the fights I had to fight? Did they know I did not choose a convenient relationship? I wanted this because I was in love with that person and shared something I was sure that I would not find with any other person in the world. And what the hell was 'normal' supposed to mean? I found it wildly derogatory.

The next months – even years – were not easy. My feelings were quite chaotic, except for the fact that I knew this was something I wanted; this is the person I wanted it with. This is the person I love and I will not find anyone else I want to share my life with. My good, my bad and my ugly.

I found it hard that there were no examples of people I knew, even in pop culture, that had a similar story to mine. I was so enthusiastic when the German production Coming In came to the movies. It is the story of a successful gay hairdresser who realises he falls in love with a girl.

It is not about the gender; it is about the person. In a parallel universe I am probably having a happy marriage with a guy. In this life – in my life – it is a gal.

After half a year of dating her, my Italian friend asked me if this was something I did for religious reasons. I knew it was not. He asked me if we even had sex. I told him we did. He nodded: 'Curious. Very curious. Well then, all the best.' We are still good friends. And I am exceedingly grateful to him for teaching me the value of acceptance and self-esteem.

We moved to east Germany where I made a couple of new friends. We would often go to hang out in bars in Berlin. They had all kinds of LGBTQ+ backgrounds. Closeted and out. No one judged. I met that one friend who was openly bi. After researching why different people identify as bi, this was something that resonated with me and I felt comfortable with.

I still hear my friend Miriam squeaking: 'Oh myyy, you are bisexual – this calls for a drink.' She raised her hand to get the cute bartender's attention: 'You know what – I am bisexual too.' I nodded along – she never made a secret about it. She kept talking: 'Isn't it awesome to have all this variety of people to be attracted to? And you know what the best part about this is? Even if you are in a relationship – you are allowed to look at the whole menu, even if you choose not to pick.' She smiled.

I am still married to the girl I got to know all those years ago back in our little student apartment. We began travelling together, started a family, and experience all the joys and struggles that probably all relationships, straight and queer, are going through. I, for my part, am still religious, still attracted to girls and guys, and I am still in love with the person I chose to live my life with.

I wish that religious communities would live the love they are preaching and integrate people of all backgrounds into their groups. I wish that being queer and being religious wouldn't exclude each other. I wish that everybody would meet a couple of special people in their lives. I wish everybody had friends who supported them; made them belong. Especially if one is not sure where exactly one does belong.

WHEN THE CURTAIN FALLS

by Agnieszka Checka

CONVERSATIONS OVER DINNER always morph into debates about the partitions, communism, or both. Our plates, cups and saucers are a translucent orange, and I watch how the light reflects off of the glass as I listen. Even though all of it feels familiar, comfortable, I start to sit with one of my legs sticking out from under the tablecloth, towards the foyer. Half at the table, half ready to leave.

'When the Russians asked about family history, you had to lie, you just had to. They wanted to wipe out the intellectuals, of course'; 'If it wasn't for Solidarity in Gdańsk, the Berlin Wall would've fallen a lot later'; 'Once you see tanks on the street on your way from school, you never forget it.'

Polish people often perceive themselves as simultaneously the heroes and martyrs, always the underdogs, always feisty. In 1795, we were picked apart and wiped off the map for over 100 years, but our national identity, culture, and heritage survived. We fought the Germans and the Russians, and we often lost, but when we did, it was always with grace

and pride. Against all odds, we were the first to start dismantling the Soviet Union. We suffered a lot, but we're proud of
it, I learn. *Bóg, honor, ojczyzna* translates to God, honour, home-
land. As I grow up, people start calling me feisty, too. It gives
me a sense of belonging.

Jesus is staring us down from his cross, hanging above the
kitchen door. Another Jesus keeps him company, guarding
the foyer. My family isn't religious, so this is hard to explain.
My grandparents' house looks very different from my
mum's, and I wonder how different my own home will be
in the future.

No one in middle school is LGBTQ+. To be queer means
to be invisible, to fold into yourself and hope no one notices
your weighty silence, a silence encouraged by a system meant
to intimidate those who are different. We see queer people
misrepresented, stereotyped and demonised in the mouths
of our politicians, our teachers, our priests, sometimes our
loved ones. As we grow older, we recognise this and start to
tend to our wounds. Heroes and martyrs.

I'm 15 the first time I kiss a girl. It happens in a closet, which
is too on-the-nose for fiction, but teenagers have a talent of
putting themselves in symbolic circumstances by accident.
I leave the party wearing both of my shoes and lose one in
a field on my way home, running from the police, stepping
in mud and laughing until there is no air left in my lungs. I
don't go looking for the shoe the next day and tell Mum a
friend's dog chewed it up. I know she knows it's not true, but
at this point it is the best explanation I can offer.

And then I'm at dinner, and I sit with the memory still
fresh in my mind. I know it was supposed to be platonic, *just
for fun, for the boys*. I look up to see multiple Christs looking
down at me, stoic and cold. I think about the plates, cups
and saucers, and about the many years they spent in my

grandparents' kitchen cupboards before I was born. They carry so much history, and so does everyone at the table. A deep sense of shame weighs down my stomach.

The year 1999 marks ten years since the start of the Third Polish Republic, eight years since the fall of the Berlin Wall, and four years since I had been born. Before the turn of the century, my mum decides to open a school that teaches foreign languages in the evenings. I am her first pupil. She encourages me to keep at it year after year, first a stubborn child, then a grumpy teenager. She tells me to speak English when we're on holiday in Egypt and I'm too embarrassed to order ice cream. She suggests I try reading the new *Harry Potter* book in English. She encourages me to watch English-speaking films. She believes in my abilities and while I don't, I trust her.

Skins is the first TV show I watch in English without subtitles, buried under the covers in my sofa bed. At 14, I am surprised to see that teenagers in Britain live in narrow houses with carpeted stairs and washing machines in their kitchens. I learn that they eat roast dinners, baked beans, and that they spend most of their time doing drugs, running down quaint streets at night, or having sex. This both scares and excites me. I want to be like them. I see their bedrooms, decked out in fairy lights and posters, and I mourn that I'm not allowed to have either of those things at home.

When I see the characters Naomi and Emily together, something locks into place. The scene that stays with me throughout the years is set in a bedroom with soft lighting, pink and orange, messy but cosy. They're close, so close. I am so enamoured I can smell the detergent on her sheets and I can taste the sweetness of another girl's lips and I'm dizzy and hope my mum doesn't wander into my room unannounced.

Without British and American TV shows, and Internet

culture, I would've seen myself absolutely nowhere, and felt, more so than I did, completely alone in my fragile newly-found sexuality. My mum opened the world to me and allowed me to understand myself in a broader context. I think it saved my life.

I come out as bisexual in a casual conversation in university halls in Glasgow at the age of 18. It is my first time saying it out loud. The word fits well in my mouth and makes me feel at home even though I'm 2,000 miles away from the only place I've ever called home.

I go to my first gay club at the age of 19 and this is where I witness a proper same-sex kiss for the first time. I look around and see another couple, and another, and another. Suddenly, I'm all flashing lights and adrenaline, I'm doing Sambuca shots, the music crawls into my ears and makes my skull vibrate. I feel numb, as if I have left my body, but in a good way – it's freeing. I am eyes and ears and lips, lips on lips, we kiss. I give myself in.

The idea of flirting with women appeals to me. I like being the pursuer. Later in the night I start chatting to someone I meet at the bar. I tell her I'm bisexual, and hear a cheeky 'So like half-gay, right?' and I can tell she has lost interest. As have I. I don't let it stop me from enjoying myself, but I think about her words in the morning, and they stay with me for longer than I'd like to admit.

On the 11th of November 2013, the first National Independence Day I spend living abroad, I read a headline about an incident involving a pro-LGBTQ+ rainbow monument in Warsaw. I click on the article and watch a video filmed during the rogue 'hooligan' part of the march. The camera is shaky, but the flames engulfing the monument are clear, loud, vicious. I hear the voices of hundreds of people shouting and singing obscenities. Parts of the monument fall to the pavement, lifeless and charred. I don't know what to do with my anger. It spills out of me in tears, a tension headache, a burning in my throat.

The English-speaking world has Stonewall. It has *The L Word*, Ellen DeGeneres, *Brokeback Mountain*, *Paris Is Burning*. My world, the way I saw it at the time, had none of those things. It had post-fascist dread, deep insecurities, an interdependent relationship with Catholicism, and a boner for 'traditional Polish values', often shown in contrast to values of the liberal West. *How did my sexuality emerge from a place like this?* I used to wonder, doubting myself every day, as I tried to fight the feeling of isolation from my own culture.

I see and hear stories of queer folk upsetting their families when they come out, falling out with loved ones, 'disappointing people,' getting attacked, verbally abused, ostracised. I watch *Friends* and learn that Carol had to leave Ross to be with Susan – his pain becomes a motif of the show. Over time I accept that to be queer means to both inflict pain, and to suffer.

These are the only two instances I distinctly remember hearing about LGBTQ+ people in my youth:

1. I must be in my early teenage years when my mum brings up a family friend and tells me that he's been with his male partner for over ten years. 'They're very much in love. They just don't want everyone finding out.' I nod. 'They're not sure how their neighbours would react, is all. They just want to stay safe,' she says. I picture a cosy flat in the old part of Gdańsk, right by the forest. I know they have a cat and a bread-maker, which sounds like the perfect home. I feel privileged to know their secret. It is safe with me.

2. We're watching TV, and a story about a trans person comes

on. I don't remember the details – I must've been quite young – but I do remember that it was a trans woman and a sad story. Mum explains that we should be compassionate to 'these kinds of people', because they're dealing with a lot of hurt and have to fight to feel at peace with their bodies, something we take for granted. I accept this, and I feel bad for the woman, but consider that maybe a substantial part of this 'hurt' comes from being perceived as inherently wounded.

The wider queer representation in Poland in the 2000s consisted of flamboyant and artistic white gay male celebrities. They made bold fashion choices, had unusual facial piercings, and spoke about sex in an open and brash way. They carried themselves with a loud confidence and I wondered if some of it acted as battle armour for the inevitable backlash received from the more conservative folk. Nowadays, I still worry that the only way some Poles are willing to accept LGBTQ+ people is to view them as different by default (their looks and the way they handle themselves) so it's clear who they are from the get-go. They can be kept at a distance.

I'm not sure when I had the realisation that women could be attracted to genders other than (cis) men, but, boy, was it a big one. The minimal queer representation that did slip under the right-wing Catholic overlords' radar involved polished, tropey stories of white men loving each other, and it was beautiful, but almost always sad, and always marked as 'different'.

I keep in touch with a few friends from high school. It's been years since our angst-ridden days, so it's easier to talk about them. On my way down to the Tatry Mountains in the summer of 2016, I visit a friend who moved from Gdańsk to Kraków for university.

We go over the struggles of being queer in our school environment. I recall the feelings of disgust, shame and isolation, but I notice myself resisting the fall back into those thought patterns. It's like looking into a foggy mirror. I recognise myself in the thoughts, but I can't connect to them anymore.

We move on to exchanging stories about ex-girlfriends – the mishaps, conflicts, awkwardness, but also declarations of love, great sex, gay bars, lesbian tropes. I realise I was surrounded by people like me all this time, we just didn't recognise each other. We chat late into the night in a beer garden in Kazimierz, the Old Jewish Quarter. I feel powerful, like I belong to a club where all members have this deeper understanding of one another. I take refuge in the conversation, the twinkling fairy lights and the sweet humming of a Friday night.

I'm on Skype with my grandparents and I have a girlfriend and I'm bursting with joy. I have to hide my hickeys under a turtleneck. I got a nose piercing and three tattoos, which seems to be a lot to process already, so I don't want to overwhelm them.

I start to correct my family when they ask about 'boyfriends', 'husband candidates', 'whether any boys fancy me.' I say 'people.' I go back to Gdańsk often. During one of my visits, on a walk through quiet leafy suburbia with my granddad, he asks me if I've found 'anyone special'. I am not sure if he has got the hint, but this non-gendered inquiry feels like progress. This promise adds a spring to my step and carries me home.

Not quite weightless, but lighter.

In June 2018, a year after I graduate university and almost five years since my move to Scotland, I see a tweet go viral. The capital of Poland is taking steps to celebrate LGBTQ+ month by installing a new monument. I look up the full story. I read that in anticipation of a Marsz Równości (Pride Parade, or Equality March), Warsaw has made a new installation. This one uses light that bounces off water vapour to create a rainbow. It sits at an intersection in the heart of a city which, only seven decades ago, was gutted and left to bleed out. Despite all odds, it stands strong now, learning how to tend to its wounds.

'I STILL FEEL LIKE I CAN'T QUITE BE MYSELF'

Bisexual students' experiences with invisibility, marginalisation, and exclusion within LGBTQ+ campus spaces

by Jayna Tavarez

IDENTIFYING AS LGBTQ+ can be really hard. We, as a community, experience invalidation, marginalisation, and exclusion as we navigate a heterosexist society that tells us our identities are unnatural. Fortunately, we've cultivated an LGBTQ+ community that is safe, celebratory, and inclusive, in order for us to collectively combat the hegemonic and oppressive systems that so painfully try to squeeze our queerness into rigid binary boxes. Right?

Except the LGBTQ+ community at large has proven time and time again that we are capable (and guilty!) of reproducing the same harmful systems that we claim to combat. Racism, cissexism, and classism, among other -isms, continue to permeate lesbian and gay spaces, and unfortunately, biphobia, the prejudice and oppression against people who identify as bisexual or who do not identify within the straight/gay binary, is no exception. As if it isn't bad enough that bisexuality is misunderstood and invalidated among straight communities (for example, studies show that bisexual people are evaluated more negatively compared to other groups,[1,2] and that bisexual people experience microaggressions more frequently than their lesbian and gay peers[3]), bisexual people continue to be invalidated, marginalised, and excluded within LGBTQ+ spaces.

The attitude that bisexuality is an invalid identity is common within lesbian and gay communities.[4,5] Scholars have found it stems in part from the idea that bisexual people do not 'pick a side,' maintaining access to heterosexual privilege.[1,6,7] As a result, bisexual people often feel unwelcome in and excluded from gay and lesbian communities,[8] which can inhibit them from being involved in LGBTQ+ spaces on college campuses and more broadly.

Studies show that this intracommunity conflict is significantly more hurtful and isolating than the everyday shit we get from straight people. Participants from both the 1991[9] and 2012[10] Bisexual Community Needs Assessments shared that they expected more acceptance from the gay and lesbian community. The biphobia they experience within LGBTQ+ spaces is especially detrimental because it comes from a community that shares similar experiences of marginalisation. This biphobia has proven to have negative impacts on bisexual people in multiple ways, contributing to a fragmented sense of sexuality,[3] internalised biphobia,[11] identity confusion,[12] difficulties coming to terms with and accepting their bisexual identity,[13] and cynicism toward and disengagement from lesbian and gay communities.[8,10]

Additionally, bisexual people may feel pressure to falsely claim a gay or lesbian identity in attempts to fit in,[3,14,15] avoid speaking up when falsely identified as gay or lesbian,[16,17] or choose to refrain from labels at all.[18] Bisexual people often act differently in varying contexts in order to feel included[3,8,13,19] at the expense of feeling authentic in their identity, which can contribute to feelings of shame for their bisexuality,[16] and may discourage them from participating in LGBTQ+ spaces.[8]

During my graduate studies, I worked at the LGBTQ+ Resource Center on campus, and while I knew of this intra-community tension in the larger LGBTQ+ community, I was floored to learn that many of the bisexual students I met experienced biphobia within our LGBTQ+ office. Learning this really impacted me; I mean, this was supposed to be our safe space on campus, the space where all LGBTQ+-identified students could go to feel validated and included in their queer identity during a time as formative as their under-graduate college experience. This was the catalyst of my two-year-long thesis research.

Through my research, I learned that despite often implementing programmes and initiatives to improve campus climate for lesbian, gay, bisexual, transgender, and queer-identifying (LGBTQ+) students, studies on their campus experiences show that colleges and universities con-tinue to be hostile and unwelcoming for them. Compared to straight students, LGBTQ+ students are more likely to con-sider leaving their college or university, steer clear of spaces intended to support LGBTQ+ students, and avoid being out as LGBTQ+ for fear of negative consequences from fellow students, faculty, and staff.[20,21,22,23]

While bisexual people at large face a unique type of mar-ginalisation within the LGBTQ+ community,[24,25] research on their experiences in higher education in particular confirms that bisexual college students are not exempt from these experiences, even in what should be safe LGBTQ+ campus spaces. To gauge how common these experiences actually were, I interviewed nine undergraduate college students who 1) identified as being attracted to more than one gender (bisexual, pansexual, polysexual, queer, fluid, etc.) and 2) were actively involved in at least one LGBTQ+ space (which included LGBTQ+ student organisations, LGBTQ+ centres, and other spaces that should be inclusive of LGBTQ+ students). When interviewing, I had two particular questions in mind... First, in what ways, if at all, do bisexual students report being marginalised within LGBTQ+ campus spaces? Second, how do these experiences impact their understandings of their bisexual identities and their involvement within LGBTQ+ campus spaces?

Biphobia within LGBTQ+ Campus Spaces

As a result of my interviews, I unfortunately learned that every single student experienced (1) invisibility, (2) marginalisation, and (3) exclusion within LGBTQ+ campus spaces that should have been safe spaces for them.

(1) Bisexual Invisibility within LGBTQ+ Campus Spaces

Students felt that bisexuality was invisible within LGBTQ+ campus spaces in more ways than one. For example, they noted that their LGBTQ+ spaces were demographically homogeneous, frequented predominantly by cisgender gay and lesbian students. They also felt the LGBTQ+ campus spaces to which they had access upheld very particular depictions of what queer identities should look like, and bisexuality often did not fit into those depictions. Additionally, they all noticed a lack of bisexual representation within the programming done by LGBTQ+ offices and organisations. Programmes offered were either completely exclusive of bisexuality or inadequately represented bisexuality when compared with lesbian and gay identities. Overall, they were frustrated by the lack of bisexual representation in LGBTQ+ campus spaces. They often needed to take matters into their own hands by hosting educational opportunities around bisexual identities, history, and issues, and creating bisexual-specific spaces. Basically, they felt that as bisexual students, if they wanted bisexual representation, they had no choice but to represent themselves.

(2) *Bisexual Marginalisation within LGBTQ+ Campus Spaces*

Each student identified examples of feeling marginalised within their LGBTQ+ campus spaces. They argued that they were often exposed to people, ideas, and stereotypes that challenged and invalidated the legitimacy of bisexuality – they felt 'not queer enough' and believed that the stereotypes permeating their LGBTQ+ spaces reinforced that 'bisexuality itself was never enough.' For example, one student Sierra made it explicitly clear that she identified as bisexual, but was consistently met with comments dismissing the validity of bisexuality from fellow students within her LGBTQ+ organisation. She explained how, despite the fact that she openly identified as bisexual, she was 'essentially treated as straight anyway.'

Much of the invalidation students experienced stemmed from the idea that bisexual people could more easily 'pass' as straight. Another student, Emma, noticed a stark contrast in how she was treated in her LGBTQ+ centre depending on the gender of her partner. She described feelings of 'discomfort' and 'shame' when she dated men, yet felt validated and supported by her peers when she dated women. Yet while these experiences were common for students in heteronormative-presenting relationships, they were not exclusive to them. For example, Ashlynn was targeted by similar comments despite being in a queer-presenting relationship. Comments such as 'You're going to leave your partner for a man'. So even when we're in 'acceptable' queer-presenting relationships, we still aren't queer enough.

(3) Bisexual Exclusion within LGBTQ+ Campus Spaces

Students expressed feeling discouraged from voicing their experiences as bisexual and did not feel as though their 'voice was as strong' as other members of the LGBTQ+ community or that they 'had the authority' to speak up within LGBTQ+ campus spaces. Many students, such as Emma, shared experiences compartmentalising parts of their lives, especially their relationships, in order to have a stronger voice:

> 'I would like to be able to be more open about [my relation-ships], but I feel like I can't talk about guys that I've dated... So a lot of times I keep my personal life, if I'm dating a guy, separate from the life that I have with activism.'

Students often felt excluded and policed by their lesbian and gay peers in regard to how bisexual people were allowed to show up and engage in LGBTQ+ campus spaces. For example, Casey recounted several times when he was referred to as an ally by students within his LGBTQ+ organisation, even though he openly identified as pansexual. Similarly, Rylee noticed that when they were perceived to be a lesbian, they felt free to participate within their LGBTQ+ organisation in the ways they wanted to participate with minimal push-back from other students. That changed, however, once they started dating someone who did not present as a woman. At that point students within the LGBTQ+ organisation reminded Rylee that they 'had no business being an activist unless [they were] actively dating another woman,' and instructed them to 'take an allyship position' instead. Rylee went on to describe the ways their LGBTQ+ organisation centred lesbian voices, and how often bisexual women in particular were excluded from the conversation:

'We were told we [could] only talk about the effects on our lives of being attracted to other women or femmes because "no one is oppressed for being in a heterosexual relationship." We were accused of internalized homophobia ... or being the reasons lesbians are fetishized and making lesbians look bad – that bisexual women were the reason why straight men thought that lesbians were sexually available... I never understood it, but it came up a lot... If you didn't seem like you were a lesbian, or could be confused for one, then your position was a lot weaker. Your opinion didn't quite matter as much. You were less likely to be one of authority in the group. Your loyalty to the community was more likely to get questioned. You were more likely to get accused of your ideas being part of the problem. Any time something came up, and you talked about it from the perspective of not being a lesbian, you were more likely to be told that your need to bring that up was part of the problem of why progress wasn't being made.'

Impact of Biphobia within LGBTQ+ Campus Spaces

Each student indicated that the challenges they experienced as bisexual students in LGBTQ+ campus spaces had a negative impact on them to some extent, leading to 1) internalised biphobia, 2) burnout and, in many cases, 3) disengagement from LGBTQ+ campus spaces.

(1) Internalising Biphobia

Several students described having negative feelings about their bisexual identities due to internalising biphobia they experienced within LGBTQ+ campus spaces. For instance, Emma felt ashamed identifying as bisexual. 'I still feel like I can't quite be myself within the LGBTQ+ community,' she shared, 'I'm still on the defense a little bit.' Students also felt they needed to hide their bisexual identities in order to remain engaged in LGBTQ+ campus spaces. Rylee felt that they 'weren't really able to stick up for their bisexual identity,' yet were willing to 'bite the bullet and go with it to be a part of [the] community.' Ashlynn was not open about their bisexual identity either and felt guilty for 'doing a disservice to the rest of the bisexual community as a whole by being out as a lesbian instead of out as bisexual.' Negotiating this tension caused Ashlynn a great deal of stress, especially because they felt they were contributing to pre-existing bisexual invisibility and 'hindering the [coming out] process of other bisexual people.'

The biphobia they internalised had negative effects on their understandings of their bisexual identities and challenged how their bisexuality fit within the context of their LGBTQ+ campus spaces. For example, Gabriel shared that his bisexual identity 'held him back' from getting to know other students in his LGBTQ+ centre. Other students questioned whether they had the right to participate in LGBTQ+ campus spaces as a bisexual. Sierra shared:

'It even made me question my identity as bisexual. It made me think... Maybe I shouldn't be in these groups... Should I just not identify as bisexual anymore? Am I being appropriative?'

Some students noted they didn't even openly identify as bisexual within LGBTQ+ campus spaces. They often felt more comfortable identifying as gay, lesbian, or queer instead of bisexual. Ashlynn falsely identified as a lesbian rather than bisexual in order to 'avoid the additional stigma.' Similarly, Jeremiah and Sierra felt that openly identifying as gay and queer, respectively, was much easier than identifying as bisexual. Other students, like Rylee, chose to not identify as anything, avoiding disclosing their sexuality entirely, choosing not to answer questions about their sexuality, and not correcting inaccurate assumptions about their sexuality.

The most disheartening issue, though, was how some began to question their own legitimacy... They started to accept – *and even participate in* – their invisibility and exclusion as a way to survive and be accepted in these LGBTQ+ spaces. The fact that they felt they had to adjust in these ways to feel accepted within spaces ostensibly designed to advocate for students like them shows 1) how truly committed they were to being involved in the LGBTQ+ community, and 2) how deeply they were impacted by biphobia within those spaces.

(2) Burnout

Every single student described symptoms of what social movement scholars have described as *activist burnout*.[26] Students frequently used the word 'exhausted' to describe the impact of their involvement in LGBTQ+ campus spaces. Most were deeply involved in multiple spaces engaging in activist work around diversity, inclusion, and social justice on campus. Many were involved in more than one organisation and held multiple leadership positions on campus, and as a result, they often felt overwhelmed and stretched thin.

For many, over-commitment to campus involvement related to issues like heterosexism and biphobia was directly linked to a sense of responsibility to combat bisexual invisibility, marginalisation, and exclusion within LGBTQ+ campus spaces. For example, Morgan was driven to create and maintain a bisexual-specific organisation on campus to meet the demand for a bisexual-specific space in response to the lack of resources provided by the LGBTQ+ centre. 'I needed to use my voice as a bisexual activist,' Morgan shared, 'not just as an activist.' Bisexual students were often pigeonholed into being the sole spokespeople for bisexual identities, and felt that it was their responsibility to educate about and advocate for bisexual students within LGBTQ+ campus spaces, while unfortunately also navigating the biphobia they themselves were experiencing.

As a result, several students developed feelings of cynicism and mistrust toward LGBTQ+ campus spaces. Rylee shared that the biphobia they internalised within their LGBTQ+ organisation caused them to develop 'a lot of anxiety around LGBT-oriented groups,' which 'took a lot of damage to [their] ability to trust LGBT organizations,' which is termed as *depersonalisation*.[26] Unfortunately, this depersonalisation caused many of them to distance themselves by either scaling back their involvement temporarily or disengaging permanently. Rylee was very passionate about LGBTQ+ issues and wanted to continue to be engaged with activism with their LGBTQ+ student organisation, but the biphobia, as well as the identity policing, they constantly experienced made them feel their involvement was pointless. In response to being frequently referred to as 'only an ally,' Rylee stated:

> 'Even if you don't believe them, you still kinda back off... Why try so hard for something when they don't want you? They don't want your effort. They don't want your support... So why try? I didn't feel like my voice was very necessary. I didn't feel like it was worth it for me to push for something that I wasn't really contributing that much to. I still want to try with activism in general because this is still important to me... but I didn't need to interact with those groups anymore, and so I stopped.'

Let us not forget that they were specifically chosen for this study because of their dedication and desire to engage around LGBTQ+ advocacy on their campuses. The biphobia that fuelled them to take on the responsibility of being 'bisexual activists' was ironically what burned them out.

The 'Martyr Syndrome'

For some of the aforementioned students, disengaging from LGBTQ+ campus spaces was an act of self-care against the burnout they were experiencing. However, not everyone was willing to do that, despite being fully aware that it would be best for their own wellbeing.

Several expressed conflicting feelings around balancing disengagement as an act of self-care and their sense of responsibility to their commitment to activism. Students described suffering from 'martyr syndrome,' the discouragement of engaging in self-care because self-care is seen as selfish and indulgent.[27] For instance, Mack recognised that the extremely high expectations they set for themselves prevented them from engaging in self-care to the extent they should have. 'I fully recognize that I could take a break if I needed to...like I wouldn't disappoint people if I [did],' they explained, '...but there's also something in me that's like [I] shouldn't take a break [because] there's people out there doing more than [me].' Similarly, Sierra echoed these expectations, noting that she could not 'fully bow out' because she took on the responsibility of being an activist:

> 'Even if I have to sometimes take a break or scale back, it's not like I'm going to stop being a queer woman or stop being Asian. The problems that I face as a result of my various identities are going to keep happening regardless, and to other people too... At the end of the day, these problems are ongoing, and they're not going to end or get better unless activists get to work.'

Jeremiah noted that he consistently prioritised the experiences of his peers over his own wellbeing, often forgetting to think of himself. He understood that he 'prioritized [his] leadership roles over going to school and being a regular student,' which has had an extremely negative impact on his academics, but he continued to be more invested in other students' education around diversity, inclusion, and social justice. For Emma, scaling back when she started to feel burned out came with overwhelming feelings of guilt and disappointment. She shared:

> 'It's definitely stressful for me when I hear somebody say something problematic, and I just don't have the energy to get into another debate or another discussion with somebody, so I just let it fly, but then I feel guilty about that... There is a little bit of guilt that comes with that when you're not standing up for people's rights 24/7, but that's practically impossible unless you just want to completely exhaust yourself.'

Altogether, they tended to be dismissive of their burnout, despite its negative impacts. Their bisexual identities were so salient to them that they felt it their duty to be committed to LGBTQ+ activism at all costs, even at the expense of their own wellbeing.

So Why Does This Matter?

My study began with examining 1) the ways bisexual students reported being marginalised within LGBTQ+ campus spaces, and 2) how those experiences impacted their understandings of their bisexual identities and their involvement within LGBTQ+ campus spaces. From their stories, I learned that not much has changed regarding how bisexual people are treated within LGBTQ+ spaces, confirming that bisexuality remains invisible, marginalised, and excluded. As a result, students frequently had to shift how they navigated LGBTQ+ spaces because of the conflict they grappled with between their desire to feel accepted and their desire to feel authentic in their identity within LGBTQ+ spaces that should be inherently inclusive of them.

If you've gotten to the end of this essay and still aren't convinced that bisexual invisibility, marginalisation, and – most baffling to me – exclusion is an issue in itself, consider how biphobia hurts more than just us. As I stated in Volume One, lesbians, gay men, and bisexual people reportedly make up only 3.5% of the United States population, and of that 3.5%, bisexual people make up 52%, followed by gay men at 31%, and lesbian women at 17%.[28] All of these statistics are to note that bisexual people make up a significant amount of the LGBTQ+ community. Bisexual people have played a significant role in early LGBTQ+ movements, and continue to make important contributions to contemporary activism. Therefore, bisexual people disengaging from activism does a disservice to the entire LGBTQ+ community. Ensuring that bisexual people feel safe and accepted engaging in activism is critical for the larger LGBTQ+ movement, and bisexual inclusion is critical in cultivating community and creating solidarity within LGBTQ+ spaces.

It is my hope that when you finish this essay, you challenge yourself to reflect on the following: what does our community gain by excluding such a large population of bisexual people who want to take on the exhausting task of dismantling heterosexism? How does biphobia threaten the sustainability of LGBTQ+ activist movements? How will you challenge biphobia in yourself and in your peers? And what effort are you willing to put in to cultivating safe and affirming bisexual-inclusive LGBTQ+ spaces?

YOU, YOU AND I

by Arthur Walsh

You were my closest friend
The one I trusted most
I loved you, and you loved me
And though we drove each other round the bend
When I was sick you gave me tea and toast
For I loved you, and you loved me

You were a stranger
One I didn't know at all
I needed you, and you needed something
And though I drank, despite the obvious danger
A helpless hopeless fool set for a fall
For I needed you, and you needed anything

I was twelve, or maybe fourteen
That I still can't remember
She was the one I trusted most
For you were my mother, and I was your son

I was twenty-two
It was my twenty-second birthday
He was someone I felt I needed
And I was just something, and nothing all the same

Even now I remember nothing,
And yet I can't forget
Nor can I forgive
Them? No

Myself …

SEXUAL ASSAULT IS something that is tremendously difficult to go through. And it's something that's hard to write about. It's been years since I was last assaulted, and though I can talk about it freely in company, or even in an almost academic context, writing about it is a much more impossible task for me. Because you can't speak for everyone who's been a victim, or a survivor, of rape even if you wanted to.

'You were my closest friend
The one I trusted most
I loved you, and you loved me
And though we drove each other round the bend
When I was sick you gave me tea and toast
For I loved you, and you loved me'

I was first assaulted when I was young. I'd love to give you a year, or an age, but I honestly can't remember it. Having spoken to other survivors of child sexual abuse (CSA), that's a really common thing. I didn't even remember it happening until I was 19 or maybe 20, when talking to a friend about condoms, of all things. They structured a sentence awkwardly, and it just all hit me. And I wasn't sure if it really happened, because it didn't seem real, it seemed like a bizarre dream. One of those dreams that is based in reality, seems really lifelike, but surely can't be real. Real or not, at the time, it cast everything about me into doubt. Have I forgotten anything else? Are things about me still valid? I started to question every facet of my life, my experiences, my identity...

Rape, generally speaking, isn't about sex or sexuality. It's about power or control. At least that's what I've read. I can't tell you what it was about from my point of view because I don't really understand why that would have been done to me at that age. And because it happened at such an innocent age, before I might have thought about who I was (or really known that who I felt I was wasn't the norm for a boy in a small Irish town), the revelation in my twenties made me doubt if I was really queer, or if I was just affected by the trauma of being raped at that age. While yeah, I had been out about being genderqueer for a while, and had sex with men and women a few times at that point, remembering that moment from my childhood brought me right back to that time, still an innocent kid who spent more time thinking about Banjo Kazooie than being bi or non-binary. The weeks and months ticked away, and I was too traumatised to even think about sex. I went years without having sex, and that added more and more pressure to confirm that, yes, I am queer, I'm not just making things up. I would force myself to go through cycles of downloading apps like Grindr, failing to meet up with anyone, further frustrating myself. I lowered my standards (which, if I'm being honest, weren't very high anyway) and eventually forced myself out the door to meet a man who was older than my dad. And that's when it happened again.

'You were a stranger
One I didn't know at all
I needed you, and you needed something
And though I drank, despite the obvious danger
A helpless hopeless fool set for a fall
For I needed you, and you needed anything'

I don't really remember anything about this time, either, but for very different reasons. It's not, for example, because of a subconscious process the brain goes through to protect you from traumatic events. I remember what I was wearing – a red hoodie I had bought before seeing that it said 'squad' on the back, plain blue jeans and navy boxer-briefs (with a brown trim). I remember exactly when it happened – it was about 7:30 on the evening of my 22nd birthday, because it was not yet twilight but the light was starting to fade from the day. I remember where I told my parents I was going – that I was meeting a friend of mine for coffee halfway between my house and the city on the bus route, because to tell them the truth would out me as bisexual (or gay, I'm not sure which they'd presume I was). I remember why I forced myself out the door, despite feeling subconscious dread and absolutely no attraction to this man – I was tired of letting my past dictate my present, so I just went for it. I even remember why I don't remember – he offered me a glass of wine I didn't want and knew not to take, but I took it anyway and downed it quickly. The last thing I remember before waking up, dizzy and slightly bloody in a ditch, was timidly undressing while being kissed by unwelcome lips.

'I was twelve, or maybe fourteen
That I still can't remember
She was the one I trusted most
For you were my mother, and I was your son

I was twenty-two
It was my twenty-second birthday
He was someone I felt I needed
And I was just something, and nothing all the same'

While neither of these people knew or cared about my being bi, and it didn't factor into anything that happened, it does affect how I reflect on things. There are more things that affect my view on it – one of these assaults happened a decade ago while the other one is fairly recent, one of the perpetrators was a random stranger while the other was decidedly not – but in my mind they're both the same. I've recovered from the immediate, physical effects of both, but both robbed me of certainty – certainty in my memory, certainty in my identity, certainty in my queerness. Did the assault in my teens make me resent my genitalia, and skew my gender towards being queer? Did the rape in my twenties prove that I'm not actually bi, and I don't have what it takes to navigate the intricacies of fucking men? I can't allow myself to fully believe the assault during my childhood actually happened... it did happen, but there's always a dark part of my mind that shouts 'liar' whenever I talk about it. And of course, I can't remember what happened on the evening of my 22nd birthday. Maybe I just hit my head, and stumbled out of the stranger's house, and it's this head injury that's caused my memory loss?

I can't trust my memory, but I can doubt myself.

I'm definitely, sadly, not the only person in the world to have been assaulted by both a man and a woman, and while internally both of these events feel the same, externally it has been made very clear that they aren't, so I'd like to offer some perspective on the similarities and differences between them. When talking about both of these events, people tend to refer to the latter one – the rape – and only ever brush over the former – the assault – as if it didn't happen, or it's just too difficult a topic to broach. That brings up another difference you mightn't think of: in legal terms I can't refer to what happened to me in my childhood as a rape because I, for all intents and purposes, was born a man, my abuser was a woman, and (as far as I remember) there was no penetration.

Gender, or at least perceived gender, plays a huge role in both the law and how people respond to hearing about assault. And I can't really blame anyone, because I feel it's at least partially the patriarchy in play. Despite identifying as genderqueer, I present mostly as masculine, meaning that I wear clothes that are traditionally seen as male, and I have substantial facial hair, so people regularly presume that I'm just a guy. Rape is a crime where, speaking statistically, the typical victims are women and the perpetrators are men, so I'm always afraid when I talk to people or go to support services that they won't believe me. I remember having to bring up that I was assaulted to qualify my opinion on something misguided a colleague was planning for a campaign on rape, and I could feel the doubt and trepidation around me as I spoke:

'Men can't be raped.'

'Who'd rape him?'

'How would that even work?'

'Fuck you for making this up.'

These are the things I could feel when I looked into the eyes of the various people around the table, and all are things I have actually heard people say to my face in real life. Society tells us that women simply couldn't do something like that, and because I'm 'a man' I surely would've been too strong to have let it happen, despite the obvious power dynamics at play there, and how young I was at the time. The reaction is different to the later rape because that's something a lot more straightforward, though sexual assault is not talked about enough in the LGBTQ+ community. People I talk to and people who have heard me talk about my rape generally believe me, and this brings another emotion to the table: guilt. People *believe* me when I tell them that some strange 50-something man raped me because people know men are rapists, and people believe men when they talk, without needing the full legal proceedings that they do when women talk about being raped. This is why I can't forget the patriarchy when I think or talk about what's happened to me, and why I feel guilt: because no one has **ever** asked me what I was wearing when it happened. And I doubt that, knowing exactly what I was wearing when I was raped, any of you thought any of it meant that I deserved what happened to me. At the time of writing there's a story dominating the headlines about a barrister in a rape trial instructing the jury to regard the underwear the victim wore on the night of the assault. I can't imagine that if my rape went before the jury that my navy boxer-briefs with a brown trim would be brought up in such a manner, and it's disturbing that what people wear would be brought up in such a setting, even if it is a 'lacy thong.'

That man was acquitted as well, by the way.

> 'Even now I remember nothing,
> And yet I can't forget
> Nor can I forgive
> Them? No
>
> Myself ...'

Despite not knowing the gory details of what happened to me as a kid, and despite never once bringing it up with my mother, I have largely forgiven her. And I don't know the stranger enough to know his name, never mind forgive him. And I don't blame the people who doubted me, because I'm sure there's a version of me who wouldn't believe me. The main person I can't forgive aren't my rapists, or the people who have ignored me in the street because they think I've made it all up, but myself. I can't forgive myself for the doubt over what happened, for pushing myself on my 22nd birthday, and for having a silly conversation that caused me to remember what happened when I was 12 or 14. I know I shouldn't feel guilty about this, or even about the relative ease I have in people believing me when I talk about my rape, but I still do. And I think I always will.

LET'S GO SWIMMING

One man's reflections on being gay and bisexual

by Simon Eilbeck

IT'S A FAMILIAR story: boy grows up, boy gets girlfriend, boy finds himself attracted to other boys, boy comes out as bisexual, then, some time later, boy finally accepts his *true* gay self. The path from bi to gay is smooth from being so well trod.

When I was a teenager in the 1990s, there was a common understanding that many men found it easier to come out as bi than to come out as gay. One narrative was that because bisexuality is supposedly closer to the 'normality' of heterosexuality than homosexuality is, it's easier for parents and friends to accept. It's a way of letting them down gently, as it leaves the door open to the comforting possibility that you could settle down in a heterosexual relationship. At the same time, it softens them up to the reality that you desire men, so that in time you can let them know who you *really* are.

But that's not the path I followed. I don't know whether my story will shed any light on the wider forces that shape experiences and practices of sexuality, but I hope that it demonstrates that trying to find a simple solution to complicated and intricate questions of desire is a fool's errand.

Memory can be an untrustworthy witness, and I'm well aware that my subconscious can manipulate my memories into a linear narrative when perhaps events, experiences and internal reflections didn't occur in quite so straightforward a fashion. However, this is my story as I remember it, and this is the story that informs how I live my life today, so its objective truth is, to be honest, of little importance. I suspect that a historical account of my experiences of grappling with sexual identities that was entirely accurate and included each shift in self-knowledge or self-generation would be nigh on unreadable (so count yourself lucky that I've chosen to tell you the edited version).

The year is 1981, and my dad has taken six-year-old me to the cinema on a Saturday afternoon. We go to see *Flash Gordon*, a sci-fi epic that's intensely camp and sexy. Despite my youth, I was instantly enamoured with the characters of Flash and Princess Aura. In one scene, Aura straddles Flash while he tries to work a telepathy machine, which elicits an involuntary thought-blurb: 'Oh my God, this girl's really turning me on!'

You and me both, pal. In that moment, I was what most bisexuals would argue bisexual people are most definitely not: confused. I was confused about desire itself – the representation of it onscreen and the feelings I was beginning to experience in my body – and about who or what I desired. Was it Flash or Aura? Did I want to straddle or be straddled?

The word 'confusion' can have some negative implications, but I was in a very happy and exciting place. Unburdened by labels, all I knew was that I was watching two hot people getting turned on – and it was turning me on.

I had crushes on boys and girls as I grew up, but lacked the courage to act on them. By the time I approached my twenties, I'd had a couple of girlfriends and enjoyed a lot of heavy petting, but hadn't done anything else with a partner. I was suppressing my attraction for boys and attempting to live as a straight man. I really was confused: not about my desires, but about how to act on them.

I asked myself: should I come out as bisexual? I was desperate to make a physical connection with a man, but worried that women wouldn't want me if I did. And I was worried that a guy wouldn't want to get together with someone who was also into women. A friend compounded my fears when she told me that she would never go out with a bisexual man because it would mean that she'd have twice the competition. It seemed like coming out as bi was a surefire way to stay a virgin.

Sticking with society's default straight identity was out of the question, as my desire for men was getting overwhelming. Queer identity wasn't really an option for me at that time, mainly due to my ignorance of what it might entail. I wasn't aware of the possibilities queerness presented – although I came to embrace it later.

That seemed to leave only one option: I would come out as gay. It would be the simplest solution. I'd be publicly identifying myself as sexually available to other men, thus infinitely increasing my chances of actually getting into bed with one. Being gay would also rule out the possibility of concerned family members trying to push me into a heterosexual life. It would leave no room for doubt. Sure, it would effectively eliminate the chance of sexual intimacy with women, but I thought I could live with that. At this point in my life I was looking for a monogamous partner, so why did I need to acknowledge desire for more than one gender? No, being gay seemed like the answer to all my problems.

Once I'd decided on my course, my relief was profound, and I set about the difficult process of coming out. Mum's reaction was sweet and sad in equal measure: 'Why can't you be like Stephen Fry and just not have sex?' My dad was more astute: 'You might be bisexual. What about your girlfriends?' I was emphatic in my denial. No room for ambiguity, Pops! A close female friend was more abrupt when I told her I was gay: 'No, you're not.' And yet I convinced myself, her and everyone else that I was.

My simple solution worked. Admittedly, it took me a while to work up the courage to meet anyone, as I was a full-time stoner, which hindered my self-confidence. I also experienced what some describe as internalised homophobia. I felt alienated from the popular gay culture of the time, which seemed to be composed mostly of Graham Norton, synchronised dancing to bad pop and an unquestioning preference for camp over sincerity in all circumstances. Yet I put myself out there: I attended meetings of my university's LGB group (we hadn't got round to adding the T by the mid-90s, although I'm sure we counted trans people among our members) and, on a visit to Edinburgh with the group, I got together with a devastatingly beautiful young man. He drove me home, we went to bed and it felt like coming home. Or maybe it just felt like coming. Either way, it was delightful; playful and a massive relief.

My decision to opt for a gay life had been validated. Although my first gay relationship was short-lived, it gave me confirmation that sharing sexual and emotional intimacy with men could be the source of *a lot* of pleasure. Enough pleasure, surely.

That's not to say I didn't have my doubts about my identity. Like many young people, I didn't want to be defined and limited by my desires. Despite the relief that I felt on discovering that sex and relationships with men would give me the pleasure and comfort I craved, my gay identity never fitted as snugly as it seemed to on others.

At university I was privileged to learn about queer theory, which offered me a different perspective on sex and identity: one in which what or who you desired, and how you acted on your desires, took precedence over who you *were*. To me, it was the key that unlocked the gilded cage of essentialist sexual identity and gave me a new way to conceptualise and understand how I was living my life. I devoured *Anti-Gay*, a collection of essays edited by the irritatingly hot curmudgeon (and former *Attitude* editor) Mark Simpson, and adopted the title of one of its chapters as a motto: 'I am not what I am'. I took comfort in transience and fluidity.

I began to think of myself as queer. It fitted. It allowed for a multitude of varieties of desire, and, just as important, it was *radical*. Queerness was based on a rejection of heteronormativity, and that made it inherently exciting to me. It opened up a space for otherness to be rebellious and fun.

Unfortunately, although queerness offered space for my desires for men and women to coexist, in practice things weren't quite so straightforward. As far as I could see, when the majority of people talked about queer men (including queer men themselves), they meant gay men. In popular culture and among friends, queer was always used as a synonym for gay – a more radical, anti-establishment version of gay, but not one that included bisexuality.

It wasn't even that it wasn't allowed – it was more that the possibility that a queer man could desire women was literally inconceivable. Nowadays people call this 'monosexism' – the pervasive assumption that human sexuality is limited to attraction to one gender. It's a powerful force, and it certainly influenced me. Through my twenties and thirties I continued to have thrilling, fun, frustrating, satisfying and sexy relationships with men, and my desires for women were shunted to the back of the cupboard, left to gather dust.

I unintentionally colluded in the suppression of my desires. I was firm in my conviction that sexuality was more about desire and behaviour than identity, so when I came out to people, I didn't say, 'I'm gay'. I preferred to let people know that I had a boyfriend (and later a husband). If they chose to assume I was gay, that was their problem – or so I told myself.

The reason for that is more subtle than simple internalised biphobia, or fear of a biphobic reaction. For me, it was as much about *easiness* – not wanting to turn a carefree conversation into something as significant and loaded as the process of coming out. As anyone who does it knows, coming out takes loads of energy and courage, and although it can result in feelings of profound relief and joy, it's still a massive pain in the ass. I can easily forgive my younger self for taking the easier option in those situations. So, out of a mixture of pragmatism, convenience, laziness and, undeniably, a little fear, I carried on living life as gay.

In my early thirties, I got together with Sergio – a handsome and warm-hearted fellow. He knew from the start that I fancied women and wasn't bothered by that. We moved in together. We looked out for each other. We were vulnerable and generous with each other in our physical intimacy. We became part of each other's families. We held hands in the street, eliciting abuse and disgust from some and smiles and admiration from others. We submerged ourselves in the comforting and rejuvenating bath of our love.

I started a club night – it's called Hot Mess. I had been inspired by queer club nights such as Horse Meat Disco, Homoelectric and Glasgow's Utter Gutter, at which I'd had the pleasure of DJing a few times. I wanted to create a space where queer kids could feel free to dance and make out with whoever they wanted to. I wanted to make the kind of party I'd always wished for when I was younger, playing music that you didn't really hear on the mainstream gay scene in Scotland.

I called Hot Mess a 'gay disco party'. That subtitle looked cool on the posters, which more often than not featured pictures of hot men in their underwear. My intention with the posters was to get in people's faces and generate responses of arousal, confusion or anger – or maybe all three. 'Gay' was still being used to mean weak or rubbish, and I was keen to use the word publicly in a way that was positive and unapologetic. By combining the phrase with undeniably sexual pictures of men kissing, I also wanted to underscore the fact that sexuality is sexual. Ten years ago, much of the debate and culture surrounding sexual identity seemed almost to ignore the reality that, rather than being an expression of some innate essence, our sexual identities are a result of desire and action. Maybe people think it's easier for straight society to accept queer people if they don't have to think about them actually having sex with each other – they might well be right. But I wanted Hot Mess to be a place where people could revel in the physicality of their queerness, so sex was central.

Hot Mess reinforced my gay identity. Although my close friends knew that I found women attractive, I felt at home as a gay man. It was an identity that felt solid and all-encompassing. I felt like part of a community – a hot, rebellious and strong community.

As Hot Mess grew in popularity, Sergio and I moved in together, and then we got engaged. This shift in our relationship had a surprising effect on me. I was happy and relieved that such a good man wanted to commit to spending the rest of his life with me, but I knew that I couldn't make a commitment that meant I would never be sexually intimate with anyone else.

Not long later I developed an intense crush on a woman. I was shocked, and once again my gay identity no longer seemed quite so comfortable. I was getting tired of trying to make it fit.

I was in my late thirties at this point, and becoming keenly aware of my mortality. I was scared of having terrible regrets when I reached the end of my days. The prospect of lying on my deathbed, wishing I'd had the courage to act on my desires, was terrifying. You only live once, right?

So I had one of the most difficult conversations I've ever had, and Sergio and I agreed to have a non-monogamous relationship. Opening up our relationship was difficult, scary, exciting, fun and rewarding. I shared hot times with friends old and new, and took great delight in connections full of exhilaration and intimacy – temporary intimacy, but no less valuable for that.

However, I found it easy to meet men for sex, but I didn't know how to begin approaching women. I didn't want to come out again, so I continued to let all but my close friends think of me as being gay – for the sake of easiness.

I realise that what I'm about to say goes against everything that a 'good' bisexual is supposed to be, but when I did decide to come out as bi, the reason was this: I realised it was the only way I was going to find sexual intimacy with women. It wasn't because I needed to express or release my 'true identity', but because I needed to act on my desires.

And it worked. The fear and excitement of coming out again gave me the impetus to act. When I finally got together with a woman, it was fun, intimate and hot. I delighted in how different a woman's body felt from a man's, and the new mechanics of sex were fascinating and awe-inspiring. And alongside the joy of making a mutually exciting connection with someone new, I felt a profound sense of relief.

A few months later I joined Tinder. My profile stated that I was in an open relationship, and my matches were scarce to say the least. However, after a few weeks I matched with Maddie. Her profile indicated that she was interested in queer feminist thought and non-monogamy, and she asked me out on a date. Before accepting, I explained that I was married to a man. I fully expected that to be the end of things, but to my surprise she told me that, rather than being put off, the fact that I had another partner was really appealing, as she wasn't a fan of the traditional heteronormative relationship model (to put it mildly).

I couldn't quite believe it. Here was a witty, attractive woman who seemed interested in me, even knowing that I was bi. When we met up, we hit it off, and we started seeing each other regularly. I was overcome with a giddy sense of *lightness*. I started to really appreciate how heavily I'd been weighed down, over decades, by the assumption that there was no way that women would ever find me attractive. My perception that my desire for men was a barrier to sexual intimacy with women slowly faded away, like a ghost who's been relieved of its haunting duties. Sure, things could still be complicated, and having two partners hasn't been simple (although thankfully Maddie and Sergio get on like a house on fire), but the feeling of joyful self-acceptance was worth the hard work.

The older I get, the more I realise that simplicity isn't all it's cracked up to be. I'm wary of anyone who tries to sell simple solutions to complex problems. People who are completely sure of themselves and appear to have no self-doubt give me the heebie-jeebies. Trying to see the world of human experience in terms of simple black-or-white binaries just makes my eyes sore.

Hot Mess is no longer a gay disco party – it's a queer dance party, and all the better for that. I've not experienced any biphobic reactions from people who knew me as gay; on the contrary, I've been pleasantly surprised by how many friends have opened up to me about their own bisexual feelings. I wonder how different my life would have been if I had known any openly bi men when I was younger.

Sometimes I miss being gay. I miss the instant feeling of community, rebelliousness and defiance that comes with being gay in a straight world. But I don't regret stepping out of my gay identity. Its contours no longer fitted my ungainly frame, and the seams had frayed so much that it would have fallen to bits sooner or later. My bi identity fits me nicely, although the day may well come when it's time to hang it up and find some new clothes.

Rather than trying to minimise complexity, uncertainty and flux in myself, I'm embracing it. I don't think I would change anything about my past, but it feels like in my younger years I was building a house on sand. The tide was always there, lapping away at my foundations, and I'd work hard to fight it. But eventually I let it go. The sea was always going to win. Rather than struggle to stay dry within my simple house on the beach, I figured I'd be better off learning to swim.

COMING OUT IN MY THIRTIES

by Sharan Dhaliwal

*NATASHA WAS BEAUTIFUL and tall – a young aspiring catwalk model who took a liking to me. I was blown away by the attention, but I didn't understand why it meant so much. We sat in the library in Hounslow Treaty Centre, when she grabbed my hands and ran her fingers over them. 'You could be a hand model, your hands are beautiful.' I looked into her eyes and melted. I wasn't listening to what she was saying, her fingers were still running over my hands and my heart beat so hard I couldn't hear anything else. I knew her through *Jason, the popular boy at school who I would sneak out of my house in the middle of the night to go see. She would see him sometimes too. We didn't talk about what we did, but the three of us knew. Jason wouldn't tell anyone at school about us – he was popular, I was far from that. But Natasha was even more secret. Our stolen glances, holding hands in the park, stroking her soft thin brown hair – I could never tell anyone.

---

* names changed for anonymity

*Sally was one of my closest friends for a while. We both knew twin brothers who lived on my road. But the nights we shared together meant more to me. At first it was considered experimental (I never told anyone about Natasha), but I soon realised she meant more to me than just comparing body hair and secretly touching each other's bodies in the dark.

'I never knew about the word gay until I came to the UK.' My family sensed something and felt the need to make these kinds of announcements. I never knew what bisexuality really meant and would laugh about how they were 'greedy' – not settling on just one gender. You were either gay or straight – anything else was ridiculous.

According to my family, anyone with a piercing who clearly smelt of cigarettes was a freak and therefore a lesbian. A lot of female friends were chased out of my life. I became one of those girls who wasn't 'like other girls', even though... I liked other girls. Men filled the void and I became the 'tomboy' in the group – a problematic term I embraced to escape my sexuality. I found it difficult to be around women without feeling shame. I looked on Facebook and wondered why all my friends had a large group of close-knit girls they hung out with, but I didn't. I found comfort in internalised misogyny.

I needed to explore my sexuality and understand it, but I felt like I couldn't. I had been told so many times that liking the music I liked was 'freaky', that chopping my hair so short made me 'look like a boy' and when I said my idol was Sarah Connor in T2, I was told she was 'too manly'. Ten years of suppressing any feelings I had towards women had taken its toll on me. I suffered from anxiety, panic attacks, depression, body disorders, and, as I realised now, a lot of bewildering sexual experiences. Maybe I would be a different person if I had been allowed to consider my sexuality, instead of being told that I had to get married to a 'good Indian boy'.

One of my biggest and longest-standing crushes has been Shannyn Sossamon, hidden under the guise of a 'girl crush'. I would cut my hair like her, dress like her and watch her films over and over. 'It's a girl crush!' I would insist. A girl crush. My friends all had girl crushes, unaware that they were allowing me to hide a secret under their thinly veiled homophobia. But I was obsessed. I would talk about Shannyn all the time – I couldn't rationalise my obsession to my straight friends and I wasn't allowed to explore why, so eventually, I suppressed her too.

I would dare myself to come out by asking friends: 'Who are the top five hottest women?', waiting for them to ask me, so I could announce Shannyn Sossamon and then explain why. I wanted to break down and tell everyone how important she was. Most times I ended up saying 'Oh, you know! The usual! Uh, Scarlett Johansson, I guess,' and sometimes I'd say Shannyn's name and mumble quietly, while showing people photos of her and trailing off into a different conversation.

I met this Greek girl at university who I fell for. She had high cheekbones, was quite thin, almost comic character-like. The way she dressed reminded me of the comic book character Chamber (who I was also in love with), but I couldn't say anything. I can't imagine many friends actually discriminating against me or treating me differently. All I could feel was irrational fear. I barely spoke to her or hung around her, but clearly remember the day she came to my halls to give me mushrooms. I showed off by taking far too many and walking to Wetherspoons at 8pm, off my face, smiling at everyone who walked past me, just because I wanted to impress the Greek girl. She never really spoke to me after that and I was forced to forget her. But you never really forget them. Like I'll never forget Antony or Will – important people in my life who have made me who I am. The difference is I was allowed to explore my feelings with men; I've never allowed myself to accept women.

On 6 September 2018, India scrapped the section of Article 377 that criminalised gay sex – introduced in 1864. The law was brought in during the rule of the British Raj to criminalise sexual activities 'against the order of nature'. It included sex with minors, bestiality, and non-consensual acts, but in 2018 the element that referred to homosexual sex was removed. This was a victory for the LGBTQ+ community in India, and in turn, globally. Our celebrations didn't stay limited to our friends; they reached out to a whole country and our families. The conversations were able to change in households – 'It's not illegal, it's not wrong.' Despite the inevitable 'It's always wrong, I don't care what people say' comments, we have comfort in the fact that our brothers and sisters back in India can live that little bit more freely.

I've only been in 'heterosexual' relationships. I was even engaged, but I hadn't been able to commit to one relationship until I finally confronted myself. I've spent the last couple of years softly whispering to selected friends, 'I'm bisexual,' but I wasn't able to yell it out loud.

I'm now 34 and finally able to say vocally: I'm bisexual and I don't feel scared anymore. Through communicating shared experiences, making friends in the community and going to QTPOC nights, I found myself immersed in a world I didn't want to leave behind. I couldn't allow myself to revert back to keeping quiet. I finally feel like some family members may be able to come to terms with my bisexuality since Article 377 was scrapped. I feel a lot more comfortable living my life as loud and proud as I want.

BI, SINGLE, AND READY TO MINGLE

Why representation of bisexual dating matters

by Katie Scott-Marshall

I DIDN'T COME out as bisexual until I was 24, when I felt safely removed from my small, inward-looking hometown in the north of England. At the school I attended growing up, nothing was considered to be more degrading or humiliating than a homophobic rumour or insult. I always knew I had a romantic and sexual interest in both men and women and my formative experiences in that arena took place with both men and women, but it took years for me to consciously identify as 'bisexual', and longer still to feel comfortable publicly identifying as such. As is the case for many confused bisexual women growing up, this was in no small part due to the fact that because I was attracted to men, and because heterosexuality is the default orientation society allocates to a cisgender woman like myself, it was easy to self-erase my queerness.

This self-erasure was made easier by the lack of representations of bisexuality in the media at the time. Growing up in the 90s and early 00s, I was aware of very few bisexual characters in film or television beyond questionable depictions in The L Word and Buffy the Vampire Slayer. Most memorably for me, the TV series Sex and the City was brutal in its treatment of bisexuality, with the female protagonists at one point debating the merits of dating a bisexual man and ultimately asserting, '[bisexuality is] just a layover on the way to Gaytown,' and that '[bisexuals should] pick a side, and stay there'. There was significant bi-erasure in the show, too, with Samantha's character temporarily identifying as a lesbian while in a romantic and sexual relationship with a woman before returning to identifying as straight.

In recent years, television has been blessed with a number of bisexual characters; perhaps most famously, Jack Harkness in Doctor Who and Torchwood, although other favourites of mine include Gillian Anderson as Stella Gibson in The Fall, and Ilana Glazer as Ilana Wexler in Broad City. However, in 2018 two shows caught my eye in particular, not only for their focus on bisexuality but specifically for their interrogation of what it is like to be bisexual and single/dating: the reality dating show The Bi Life (ongoing at the time of writing, and presented by Australian drag queen Courtney Act), and the television series The Bisexual (written, directed by, and starring the multi-talented American-Iranian Desiree Akhavan).

The Bi Life has a well-intentioned concept; in its simplest form it is a reality dating show that focuses exclusively on a group of bisexuals sharing a house in Barcelona and going out on dates. The group report back to one another and bond by sharing and comparing their dating experiences. Unlike similar shows, the participants aren't competing against one another for money, or under pressure to couple up to generate sensationalism and ramp up the viewing figures, which is refreshing and makes the content comparatively wholesome. However, the design of having a 'little hermetically sealed microcosm of bisexual people', as Courtney

Act describes it in a promotional interview, still stirs in me some discomfort. There is a sense of the group being show-cased and put on display for the benefit of others' curiosity and in order to repeatedly dispel myths about bisexuality as they date monosexuals. A bisexual friend texted me after watching the pilot episode to say, 'I'm so sick of queer love having to be filtered through an "educate the heterosexuals" gaze [...] I don't exist for others' consumption'.

In *The Bisexual*, too, the character Gabe seems to exist pri-marily in order to feature a heterosexual perspective that can be repeatedly educated for the wider benefit of the audi-ence whenever he vocalises ignorant assumptions about bisexuality. Perhaps the most obvious of these is when his character says to Leila (the protagonist, played by Akhavan) that as a bisexual she is lucky not to have to worry about romantic relationships because 'monogamy's not possible for you', causing her to nearly cry and refuse to share a taxi home with him. Certainly, one of the biggest preconceptions of bisexuality that I have found myself battling with others on is the idea that bisexuals are attracted to an unlimited number of people, and therefore incapable of monogamy. Frustratingly, *The Bi Life* doesn't challenge this stereotype, with one woman on the show actively saying that as a bisexual she has 'more choice', and this being included in the recap at the beginning of every episode. This is a damaging miscon-ception that contributes to the problematic assumption that bisexuals are naturally more inclined to be promiscuous or interested in polyamory just by virtue of being bisexual, and the conflation of bisexuality with hypersexuality.

In reality, being bisexual may sometimes, but by no means always, increase your options when single and looking to date. I have many straight female friends whom I would ven-ture to say are attracted to a higher percentage of the general population than I am, despite them only being interested in one gender. Individuals have personal preferences, after all, and as the bisexual YouTube lifestyle blogger Melanie Murphy wryly puts it in one of her videos discussing what it is like to date as a bisexual, '[I'm] very picky when it comes to who I actually put my face on'. This point is underlined in The Bisexual when Leila has a confrontation with her ex-girlfriend in the season finale after Sadie (portrayed in a revelatory performance by Maxine Peake) accuses her of being unable to 'be fully satisfied' in a relationship with one person as a bisexual. Leila articulately counters that 'no person can give another person all the things they need', and that 'monogamy is monogamy [... my attraction to men] didn't matter, I was in love with you'.

When I first moved to London and tried my hand at online dating, I was nervous. On OKCupid, I listed my sexual orientation as bisexual, but tried narrowing my search preferences to just men, thinking that this would be an easier transition into online dating, as I had only recently come out and found the idea of dating men less intimidating (although even now, I shouldn't have to justify this). The app automatically and forcibly reverted my sexual orientation on my public profile to 'straight' when I tried to tailor the search options. This is grossly unfair and discriminatory on multiple levels, and is a key example of how bi-erasure permeates dating apps.

It's also an anxiety specific to our times and to dating in the 21st century, which The Bisexual goes some way to examining through its depiction of Leila trawling through dating apps and also through an acknowledgement of generational gaps in dating experiences. Gabe's character dates a 22-year-old who asks Leila why she is struggling with coming out as bisexual when she has already spent a long period of time identifying as gay, asking, 'So [what if you're bisexual]? I'm queer'. Leila retorts that 'Everyone under 25 thinks that they're queer'. She goes on to explain that coming out as gay was so traumatic for her that to now come out as bisexual would feel like an insult: 'When you have to fight for it, being gay can become the biggest part of you [...] you can't do both.' Her dismissiveness of the younger generation is ironically echoed back at her through her ex-girlfriend, who is a decade older than her, shouting at her that she has no 'idea what it's like to be a dyke growing up in Burnley in the 80s'. In this way the show brilliantly exposes the tensions underlying generational differences in dating as someone queer.

Leila's character also struggles with coming out as bisexual due to an internalised biphobia that is perpetuated by the lesbian community she was originally a part of; one where lesbian characters in the show refer to bisexual women as 'sex tourists'. It is refreshing to see a show exposing the sad fact that biphobia and discrimination isn't just levelled against bisexuals by heterosexuals, but also by some members of the gay community. Even in my experiences outside of dating, I have encountered gay women who have disputed whether bisexuals should be equally welcome at Pride events and had heated discussions with gay women about bisexual visibility. As Akhavan stated in an interview, 'You identify [bisexuals] according to whose hand they're holding in that moment.'

I found The Bisexual's examination of internalised biphobia fascinating because when I said at the start of this essay that at my school, homophobia was rife, I don't just mean that it was terrifying to be a queer kid in that institution because other kids were homophobic. If you were queer, you internalised that homophobia too. I had a relatively easy time of it at school compared to many of my peers and was lucky to have a tight-knit group of friends that I remain close with to this day, but there was a short period of time when I was 13 where an unfounded rumour circulated that I was gay. For months I dreaded going to school, dreaded getting changed for P.E., and dreaded walking home. I can recall each homophobic remark made to me with unnerving precision and accuracy over a decade later. One girl refused to partner with me on a project, resulting in us both being kicked out of the classroom; interestingly, she came out as a lesbian as an adult, and I don't think the fact she was the most aggressive towards me is a coincidence. She had internalised the homophobia too.

Because I present as feminine, I wasn't at risk of boys being violent with me in the same way many androgynous and masculine queer women are, but the threat of sexual violence and level of sexual interest and harassment I received from teenage boys did increase amidst the rumour. I never told my parents that I was being bullied, convinced that I had to starve the rumour to death by remaining silent. I did this so effectively that when I have mentioned this time to school friends, they have had little to no memory of it ever happening.

I silenced that rumour by silencing myself and a part of my identity. I realise in hindsight I was scared that if I told my parents, they would believe the rumour too. I was also afraid of my friends believing it and thinking that I was attracted to them when I wasn't. However, my indignance not only stemmed from internalised homophobia: it was also the fact that I wasn't gay. I was bisexual. The problem was that I couldn't articulate this; I just knew that I had a definite interest in men and that no one would believe that was true if I admitted to any interest in women as well. This is crucial in understanding biphobia. The legitimacy of bisexuality as an orientation is constantly undermined by a potent combination of homophobia and bi-erasure.

Despite some of the criticisms I have levelled against The Bi Life – and it is important that we critically interrogate any and all representations of LGBTQ+ communities and continually strive to do better – I can't help but think that if a popular dating show like that had existed when I was a teenager, perhaps there would have been less viciousness and fear towards queerness among my peers, especially as my school was largely white and working-class and therefore a target demographic audience for British reality television. The Bi Life should also be lauded for its inclusion of a number of bisexual men, who are often painfully absent from discussions of bisexuality.

History shows us time and time again that people fear what they don't understand, and that empathy is at the root of compassion. Popular culture is one of the most simple and effective vehicles by which to embed new ideas and promote diversity, and to engage people in narratives where they can sympathise with people who are different to themselves. Being single as a bisexual and dating as a bisexual can be an exhausting experience, in no small part because of the energy that bisexuals have to expend educating monosexuals in the ways I have discussed, but also because the future is far less predictable in terms of what kind of relationships you might end up embarking on. Surely, it's a time of cautious optimism to see bisexuality being explored in the media as a valid orientation, and to see single bisexual individuals navigating the worlds of both queer and straight dating and exploring their sexualities freely. These are individuals with distinct personalities that are defined by more than who they go to bed with: ultimately, this visibility is important, both for the solidarity it affords bisexuals and the education it provides.

MYSTERIES OF EROS

A pansexual awakening

by Robert J. Holmes

EVERYWHERE YOU LOOK there are strangers, no reflections of yourself.

Except, perhaps, one person. A girl.

There's always a girl. When the Doctor is asked by Winston Churchill, 'What happened to time?' the response was, 'A woman'. Luke Skywalker could not have become a Grand Master without Mara Jade – the woman hellbent on his death, at least until they fell in love.

This girl, she was a bit of a 'tomboy'. Nerdy, always playing video games, ready to rough and tumble, and chancing on getting served alcohol at 13 because she looked much older. One of the lads, you might say.

And if you're gay, it was the stereotypical friendship.

Friends and family always joked you'd end up together one day. Strangers would mistake you for brother and sister. You'd agreed on fake names for each other, in case strangers got too friendly in town, where every Thursday after school you'd go and browse the comic book stores.

She was the only one you could talk to.

You can tell people so much about yourself – yet, never how you feel about those things. Never stopping to interrogate why you feel the way you do; what can be done better. With her you asked questions; probed each other's depths. You cared to get to the heart of things, to what gnawed away at your heads and hearts. It was reciprocal, flipflopping like lovers. Active. Passive. Gushing breathlessly.

You'd stay up til 3am drinking wine, putting the world to rights, singing until your throat hurt.

She was your safe space.

She had 'balls' enough for both of you.

Sure, you had ups and downs, as every friendship does. Long stretches of time where you wouldn't speak because you both felt let down by the other.

If you were straight, it could have been perfect; the classic high school sweethearts story.

Her yang to your yin, confessing your sins and being comforted by love.

Of course, that's never the narrative for gay men.

You don't get happy endings, or at least that's what you're taught. There are no models of how to have a healthy relationship with another guy, no clearly defined narrative arc for you to follow the script like straights can. The only script you have is the horror stories they tell you of the sad, lonely old men in bars, trying to recapture their lost youth; of AIDS; crystal meth heads; rent boys; porn addicts; drama queens; gay bashing.

The only positive you're told you're likely to get is a terminal diagnosis.

Without sign posts, you're lost. Doomed to tread the well-worn path of sad queers everywhere.

One day, everyone moves on without you. They get married, have children. She finds her beau and no longer needs you. Try as you might to keep the friendship alive, your bond is shattered by time and distance and you become shadows in the ether.

You're facing a future alone. Without your forever friend – the tempering force to your bottled rage, your guide through the shitstorms – you retreat from life, hoping to find erasure but never quite succeeding. You have no choice but to play a part, to 'be a man' and support yourself through steely determination alone. Success at the cost of a heart. There can be no room for such things as softness, playfulness, happiness.

Not with a guy, at any rate.

New friendships pale in comparison, and you present a deflated, diluted version of yourself even as an 'out' man; puff up your chest and paint a smile on as you make your way up the career ladder – aching inside, dying for something incomprehensible. You satiate it like a vampire with masturbatory material and Grindr hook-ups; you've absorbed by osmosis the attitudes of the straight men whose approval you craved. Learned to assimilate. Learned you had an inalienable right to sex, to browse men's bodies like a catalogue. That sex was sex for the sake of sex. Emotional work never factors in your calculations; you're no longer capable of adding up feelings, of finding the root of the heart.

Eventually, you forget how to be a friend.

You forget how to live. Expending so much energy trying to be someone to everyone, you neglect yourself.

So you take a breath and wake; open yourself to the zeitgeist.

When you least expect it he's there with kindling for your ashen heart, and the fire roars to life once again, passionate, intimate. Words come without conscious thought, gushing unfiltered, echoing one another in understanding. In his eyes, you see a reflection of yourself.

You laugh, dance, sing together. When you're wrapped up, you are whole. His hand phases through your barriers, touching something primal, instinctive, and the sinuous line dissolves in the poetry of your 69. Flipping each other back and forth across that technicolour spectrum between femme and masc, light and dark, balanced in perfect synchronicity. You're disarmed, alternating caresses, soft then firm. You fumble; get tired.

Afterward you lie there, fingers, arms, legs entwined. His pelvis rests gently above yours. He tilts his head up, and you trace the contours of his soft lips, his cheekbones, with your eyes. His tongue quivers uncertainly over his bottom lip, mouth forming a question as his eyes search yours for an answer. You respond with a kiss-brush, nudge his nose with yours. You both sigh, and he buries his head in your collar. For once the shame is gone, and it's like you've earned it; a peaceful reward. When he leaves, you trace the scent of a man on your sheets. On your heart, he leaves the trace of a woman.

Now you're more confused than ever before, emotions flying chaotically in every direction. As your thirties hurtle toward you with all the weight of the car crash that has been your life so far, you start to feel a twinge of bisexuality. His slight effeminacy, his receptiveness, the tenderness... You question so much you never noticed before.

It's terrifying, considering you fiercely asserted your homosexuality since coming out. Perhaps overcompensating. You start to wonder... but no. You understand that on some level you love women, you understand them, can see their struggle as like your own. You feel affection for them, could probably sleep with them if trust was there. A one-time thing, maybe. Or a couple times for the right friend. Queer theory tells you only a gay man could truly love a woman entirely, satisfy her needs in ways 'exclusively' straight men can't.*

Yet, a woman for the rest of your days? No musky man scent, no hardness against your back? No firm, flat chest to rest your head against when you're weary?

A woman in a man's body, sure. A man in a woman's body… Who knows? You're not entirely sure how that would even work.

You shudder to think, and thinking's all you seem to do these days. That and feeling just so much more. You try to drown it all out with alcohol and laughter and music, anything to lose yourself in the moment and postpone the finality of applying a label, of committing one way or the other.

You go to Pride and revel in the spectacle, party from morning to midnight. It triggers all your old personas; your confidence spikes and you feel secure. Secure enough to kiss a girl on the stage, tongue and all, and like it. Everyone's kissing and touching everyone in between passing round poppers and rubbing coke to their gums; soaking in the heady rush. The thrill of it! The wandering hands of all genders slip inside your open shirt, caressing your chest. Some lean in to kiss it, to pick at your nipples.

You're a god – the stage is your world and you own it.

Pride has its use. It's good for you to understand you're not alone in this pursuit to forget and deny, to suppress all other desires and needs except sex. You're not alone in thinking there's no meaning or feeling to anything at all. It's good

---

* Maria Mieli writes in Homosexuality & Liberation: Elements of a Gay Critique that 'the more fear a man has of being fucked, the more he himself fucks badly, with scant consideration for the other person, who is reduced to a mere hole, a receptacle for his blind phallic egoism. Someone who likes being fucked, on the other hand, will himself know how to fuck well. He knows how to give pleasure, as he knows how to receive it, and he unblocks the restricted fixation of stereotyped roles. To fuck then truly does become a relation of reciprocity, an intersubjective act.'

for you to see a whole community pathologized by wider society; to see the same patterns of behaviours and personal histories – your corrupted sexuality, shamed by religion and politics in the name of capitalism – reflected back at you. To see people wounded and unable to heal, and to know you cannot help them, because you do not fully understand yourself yet.

It's time, you think, to give it all up. The clubs and the wildness and wilderness of it all.

Maybe once a year you can make a big deal about Pride. It's always good to show your colours, to be visible and be part of the community. Yet, what happens afterward? Where does the pride go, once you get home and crash and burn, a frustrated horny mess of shame? When family calls to check up, and there's nothing good to talk about because you're too embarrassed to admit your stories, bound up as they are in a world they would rather deny and ridicule?

Where's the pride in oneself, distinct from sexuality?

Where do you go, when you're alone in your bed?

You start to ponder Hannah Gadsby's question of 'Where do the quiet gays go?'[1] You start to wrestle with and dissect your own pathology, slowly realising there's a voice you stopped listening to, one shunned in favour of those who would put you down.

A child's voice cries out for long journeys, for new places and quiet countryside hikes, and a boy's head to rest your own against. For books and more books. For freedom from having to be merely tolerated in the workplace and family, a lone voice among the monotony of hets who never adjust their stance, who can see no deeper into themselves or others than surface detail, or cling rigidly to their enforced ideals without question. He reminds you of being seven – coming out of school hand-in-hand with your best friend – and your nan proclaiming how boys shouldn't hold hands in case they might be gay.

You try to explain how he's making himself invisible by settling down to a quiet life, hidden in his cottage, reading in front of an open fire.

I'm tired, he tells you. Tired of caring, of making an effort and trying to carve out just a little bit of space in order to prove myself. Tired of being something I'm not; an intellectual, an artist, a 'man'. It's my life. I only need a few good friends. A little queer family to call my own, without the bullshit of other families. To walk down a country lane holding hands with the one who's both brother and sister, and contemplate the mysteries of Eros, of family, community and religion. I need you to give it up – you don't have to fuck every guy you can just to be queer, you know. Those other lost boys can find their own way, but I need you now. Don't be a coward, don't give in to what they expect – we deserve better than that.

As you listen to his voice, a path appears through the zeitgeist, and the wind screams adventure and possibility. Yet queer rage remains, brimming with resentment, simmering beneath the surface. There is work to be done, and it stings that you have to push harder, faster and higher than those more privileged – traumas to overcome, support networks to build, if you're ever to have the life that you want with marriage and children. There are still no sign posts, only the silhouettes of friends pointing the way; the story still unwritten.

TAPESTRIES WOVEN IN MANY THREADS

A bisexual intersection

by Rosalind Smith

SO, YOU ALREADY knew I was bi before you even started reading this. But as I started trying to write out my personal experiences with bisexuality, I found myself dealing with other integral parts of my identity that in theory I understood as separate from my sexuality. My gender, or lack of one, at least felt logically connected. But my identity as disabled, or as an abuse survivor, seemed like things that should feel separate. But they didn't. They aren't. As I tried to unwind the strand of bisexuality that runs through my sense of self, I found it inseparably woven in with other core parts of my identity – so much so that I couldn't talk about any one experience which was solely a 'Bisexual Experience' rather than a detailed fragment on a wider tapestry of identity that, to put it a less pretentious way, is just my life.

Now, before we start talking about the bisexual intersection mentioned in the title, I'm going to have to let you in on a dark little secret from my past. When I was a 14, not only was I not a feminist, I was an anti-feminist. I blame a lot of this on internalised misogyny, or having what I hadn't realised was a complicated big ol' gay crush on my then-best friend, who convinced me I had to be an anti-feminist just like her. But what made all that so easy was that mainstream feminism, in ways I didn't fully understand yet because of these threads I had no names for, was incredibly alienating for me. For some inexplicable reason, the concerns of middle-class, straight cis women's feminism never felt like they were speaking to me, or that they were supposed to be for me (the inexplicable reason being that I was none of these things, but I didn't know that back then).

So, flash forward four years, one innocence-shattering sexual assault, many 'platonic' kisses with female friends, an endless insistence that I couldn't be a lesbian because I liked men, and a brief dalliance with the word 'bicurious' that was quickly shut down, I realised that there were women out there discussing a kind of misogyny I could more readily understand. You see, I had been denying that women were oppressed in the modern era for two main reasons. The first, that admitting people hate you for reasons you can't control is terrifying. And the second, that I had not seen discussions about misogyny that resonated with my own life – and, mostly out of fear of admitting some hard truths about myself, I had actively avoided seeking these out.

But then, suddenly, here was intersectional feminism! And I found people critiquing the same issues with neo-liberal feminism that I had, but from perspectives I hadn't even considered yet, and in ways that were productive rather than just me whining about the fact I didn't feel empowered by the simple virtue of having been born with a womb, and that I was never going to have 'eyeliner sharp enough to kill a man' because my autistic ass (at this point in our story, not yet diagnosed) could not bear the sensory hell and societal pressure of make-up.

I should probably also add a little autism disclaimer before I go on as well, just so we're on the same page. Fundamentally, my brain is wired differently, and this leads to sensory processing issues, social dysfunction, and issues with processing information and executive dysfunction. I'm not going to single it out in this discussion, but by virtue of it just being a part of me and how I understand the world, it's a constant thread through my understanding of my sexuality, my gender, and my other life experiences as a disabled, bisexual, non-binary lass.

So, back to bisexuality. It's no accident that, after I found a kind of feminism that made me examine my own experiences closely, the penny finally dropped. I'd just started what was to be a slightly ill-fated attempt at a history degree, and my first ever relationship (which began somewhere in the middle of that last paragraph) was about to turn incredibly sour. I'd been having this incredible recurring dream, where I was a pirate queen coursing through the Adriatic Sea in some unspecified medieval period. But then one night, this swashbuckling seductress saved a girl from some men while they were in port, and took her back to her cabin. And that was it. I woke up the next morning with one simple thought in my head: 'Oh, girls! I'm bisexual.' And that was that.

I always like telling this story. It's fun and easy, and glosses over all of the pain. It had taken years of working out in my subconscious. It skips the years of being terrified to even look at other women (or was that the old 'eye contact is terrifying' autism trait cropping up? Who knows? I sure as hell don't). I got asked if I was a lesbian a lot, but never for the right reasons. It was because I wasn't interested in dating for most of my teens, or because I was gender non-conforming, or because I was 'weird'. It was never because what I now recognise as obvious crushes on women were being acknowledged for what they were. Might be the autism cropping up again, but eventually I could only see my attraction – to both men and women (hadn't got to dismantling the gender binary at this point) – through other people's eyes. It was no longer my own, but something I observed as separate from me, that had to be moulded into what other people found acceptable.

But when I tell this story about being a wild, adventurous bisexual pirate (or birate, as I call them), it doesn't need to be about any of that. It's just joy. The sheer joy of my sexuality, of owning it, or it belonging to me, and finally being allowed to enjoy it. Even more recently, when I had a little 'Oh, wait, what if all the attraction I've felt for men was actually just compulsory heterosexuality?' wobble, it didn't cause me pain the way agonising over my sexuality had in the past, before it even had a name. It might ignore the bits that hurt, but the moment I woke up and was hit with this realisation was a line in the sand. We all know the stereotype of bisexuals just being confused, but it was truly one of the greatest moments of clarity in my life. Everything just made sense. I'm actually very easily confused, by a lot of things, mostly maths (now there's an autism myth busted for you too, to go along with the bi one) but that moment was possibly the least confused I've ever been. Autistic people, we are told (usually by neurotypical people), dislike ambiguity, and can only deal in precise facts. It's a generalisation, often times based off of stereotypes, but in this case, it is quite true. Once my bisexuality was an indisputable fact, that was it. It became a solid truth.

I was raised an atheist, and although I don't consider myself one (my teenage rebellion was briefly becoming a Quaker), I've never really felt connected to organised religion. But I've heard people talk a lot about truth setting you free. Now, I don't understand that in the context they mean at all. But in the context of my own life, finding elements of my sense of self, my life, and my identity to be factual truths was freeing. I knew I was bi, and that was that. Never mind that I was dating a man, that I'd never had sex with a girl, or been in a relationship with one, or kissed a girl outside of the context of being drunk and doing it 'for the guys' at parties. It felt a bit like my bisexuality had been stewing away in a pot in the back of my mind, waiting to be served up once it was fully cooked and ready.

That's kind of how my gender identity went down as well. I just realised I wasn't a girl, and I wasn't a guy, and that was that. I had known that non-binary genders existed for a few years, but much like with bisexuality, it took a long time for it to feel like something I could be.

Some people do say that bisexuality excludes non-binary genders, but that feels quite alien to me, because even before I started really understanding my own gender, when I defined my bisexuality as attraction to men and women, it was only because I didn't actually know anyone else who was non-binary. So I assumed I would be attracted to people regardless of gender, but I didn't technically have any evidence of that as far as I was aware. Now of course, the idea that bisexuality could ever exclude non-binary people just seems ridiculous to me, by virtue of my own existence, and I think if I had known anything about trans and non-binary identities growing up (transphobic episodes TV shows I'd rather forget notwithstanding) this would have been obvious to me from the get-go. Actually knowing another trans person might have been a great start as well, but given that I barely knew any gay people up until the summer my entire ranger guide unit came out, that wasn't really on the cards.

Much like my bisexuality, once my gender was finished cooking in the oven of my subconscious, that was that. I referred to myself as 'a non-binary lass' earlier and I should probably clarify that. Of course, a lot of non-binary people don't feel aligned to any gender, but I feel some attachment to, if not womanhood exactly, the idea that if I had to pick a side, I'm closer to being a girl. But that might change as I get more used to my identity. I certainly hate the stereotype that bi people have to pick a side, so it should probably annoy me more that I feel like that about my gender identity. Maybe it'll get ironed out in the future, or maybe I'll always feel what I once described as 'none gender, with left girl' (because I seem to have spent this entire experience of gender discovery only able to communicate my feelings through memes). At the very least, I've never felt like my own gender excluded me from bisexuality.

There is, of course, a growing theory that autistic people experience gender differently from neurotypical people. Now, what with a sizeable chunk of my close friend group being other bi enby autistics, I might have a slightly biased perspective on this. But I do wonder how much of my enby-ness is informed by the fact that for the most part, gender is a social beast. Femininity, especially, is often more about enforced social cues and expectations that I as an autistic lass feel completely unable to tap into. A huge aspect of femininity is to do with presentation, and this can be difficult when mixed in with autism as well, as while a full face of make-up makes me feel like I'm suffocating, a floaty skirt is absolute sensory heaven. I used to worry that this meant I wasn't non-binary enough, but really, the answer to this doesn't matter to me. At the end of the day, I don't feel like a man or a woman, and that's sort of all that matters. There doesn't really need to be a reason for it. Much like there doesn't need to be a reason for my bisexuality, or my autism. You see what I mean about interwoven threads?

One thing there is a reason for (and it isn't short skirts) is sexual assault and abuse. So, this is the heavy bit here. As mentioned elsewhere in this book bisexual women are twice as likely to experience domestic violence than straight women[1], nearly two thirds of bi women have been raped, and half of those for the first time between the ages of 11 and 17[2]. I know there are lies, damned lies and statistics, but that truly is a horrifying number. But it's a reality. And it's my reality; it completely reflects my lived experience. I won't go into the gory details, but my ex used to justify what he did to me by citing the emotional strain it caused him to be dating a bi girl, because I was obviously going to cheat on him and he had to hurt me to stop me doing that. You can only laugh sometimes at the absurd logic abusers use to justify actions.

The earlier sexual assault I mentioned (really, I would call it rape, but Scots law is rather backward in this regard, and only considers it rape if a penis is inserted, but that's a rant for another time) was influenced by my bisexuality, too. If you spend your teenage years going around and kissing girls, unfortunately some people are going to call you a slut. And they're going to use that to justify treating you like an object. It's an all too common stereotype for bi women that we are innately and aggressively sexual beings, that we are easy, and down to shag anything that moves. We are seen as existing for the sexual gratification of straight men. We're their fantasy of a lesbian they've managed to turn straight (another one you've got to laugh at the nonsense of). We're the living sex toy they can pressure their reluctant girlfriend into having a threesome with. Maybe that attitude is why the statistics are so high for bi women.

I've focused particularly on violence and sexual assault from straight men, because that's what I've personally known, but abuse from women is all too often not spoken about. The worst part of coming out, for me, was my friend telling me calmly and politely that she was scared I was going to rape her in her sleep. The stereotype of Sapphic women being predatory is all too common, and fear of reinforcing this can also shut down this side of the conversation that we really need to be having. Bi women are damned no matter who we are abused by. And this is heightened by the fact that we are seen as naturally promiscuous, and therefore inviting this treatment.

When I was talking about intersectional feminism earlier, it reminded me that I used to view the intersection of different marginalised identities as a sort of stack-up points list. Maybe it's because I didn't think I had any personal intersecting marginalised identities back then, but that feels like such an outside perspective to me now. That's why I like the tapestry metaphor more. Because if I tried to pick out for you whether my sexuality, my gender, or my disability is what made me more vulnerable to that abuse, they would all be the answer.

I love folk music, and in the aftermath of that experience, when I was trapped in the limbo between abuse and recovery for about a year, I listened to Joan Baez and nothing else for about six months straight. I was led to the tiny glimmer of hope in my Pandora's box of misery by the queen of folk, who came out as bisexual herself in 1973. It was a folk song I had in mind when I finally figured out what direction I wanted to go in with this essay – Davy Steele's 'Scotland Yet', which I first heard beautifully reimagined by Karine Polwart. It discusses Scottish identity (and particularly language and culture) changing throughout time, and all manifestations being relevant.

Perhaps it's a little romantic to think of one's identity as a tapestry, but surely no more whimsical than figuring out your sexuality through a dream of being a bisexual pirate. There were parts of that recurring series of dreams that turned into nightmares, where my sleeping brain processed sexual assault that it could not yet name, could not shape into concrete facts like my bisexuality. Bi lassies can't even catch a break in our own dreams, it appears. But maybe that's why these threads are bound so tight. My understanding of my bisexuality is tied to my experiences of sexual violence – not just because it made it statistically more likely, but because it was in trying to reframe how I felt about sex and attraction after being sexually assaulted, after never having really experienced sexual attraction beforehand, let alone having had any actual sexual experience, that I opened myself up to my bisexuality. I'd have almost certainly figured it out anyway, but the experiences remain interlinked.

And when I wrote off my attraction to women as being part of a social dysfunction that I didn't even understand I had back then, well, it would have been nicer if that hadn't been how I experienced it, but it was. I think it was easier for me to consider the strands of identity as separate when I was young, and looking at the separate strands still on the edges of my loom, which vastly outweighed what had already been woven. The more I weave, the more I see identity as one whole and complex picture. A lot of people complain, in that polite sort of bigotry, about LGBTQ+ people making their gender or sexuality their entire identity. I've definitely had people complain about me doing that. But it's just one – perhaps particularly vibrant – strand that makes the tapestry all the more beautiful for being in the centre, instead of hidden away.

LAND OF THE LOST BOYS

by D. Keaney

IF YOU ARE reading this and feel lost, know you are not alone. I am writing to you to share with you an excerpt from a story I will continue to write until the day I die. Welcome to the Land of the Lost Boys.

It was sometime in my early teens that I began to feel like a Lost Boy. Was it my body consciousness? Was it the teasing about my weight I copped every day from my friends? Who knows – I mean, that 'puppy fat' weight would drop once puberty squeezed me in its awkward, acne-ridden arms, right? That's what I hoped (and it did), but till then I spent what felt like hours in front of the mirror, analysing, critiquing and picturing the perfect body, a body like the picture-perfect shirtless male models I saw online. That's where my initial attraction began; just me, a screen, and whatever perfectly chiselled body stared back at me.

I always wanted the perfect figure, and as I began to grow comfortable looking at these images online, I began to think my attraction lay solely in the idea that it was something I wanted so badly for myself. And it made sense – to me at least. Hindsight is a great thing, but as I look back now, it still makes sense. Even as I psychoanalyse my pubescent younger self, I still believe a significant amount of that attraction came from the pursuit of a better version of me; one that I was happy with. That level of reasoning mixed with the raging hormones left me well and truly shipwrecked on the lone shores of the Land of the Lost Boys.

As time went by and I ventured further into my teenage years with their end in sight, I became more sure of myself but at the same time more and more lost within the reaffirmed logic I had created. By that time, I had started going to the gym, seeing results, and day by day becoming happier with who I was. The fitness industry had taken off by now and social media was full of topless models flogging discounts left, right and centre. Still, I believed this spark of attraction I felt was no more than the 'body goals' that I aspired towards; the 'goals' that were constantly shoved in my face.

As a budding biologist in training, I theorised that men can, and did, find other men attractive and recognise them as handsome due to the biological function of 'knowing your league', your competition, and how well of a chance you stood when trying to compete for the affection of a woman. After all, my straight guy friends freely commented about how handsome other guys – or other male friends – looked, and this was a regular occurrence. Some of them had even had drunken kisses with other guys and the next day it was no big deal, just something to laugh about among the other alcohol-fuelled chaos that ensued; often involving whiskey, wheelie-bins and objects that really should not belong in a student house. Amidst it all, I was still very much lost within the shadows of the Land of the Lost Boys. Then I met 'Her'.

'She' was the catalyst and the beginning of something bigger within myself; the signpost of my new journey into the world of relationships. She was stunning, with long curly dark hair, a timeless beauty, and haunting eyes that rivalled Bambi's. She was picture perfect and, to be honest, I was never sure what she even saw in me. But I liked her, and I knew that much. Time went by and we got to know each other more and more, and soon we found ourselves tangled up in a long-lasting relationship, the details of which I will respectfully keep to myself.

Towards the end of the relationship the idea of saying the word 'love' was thrown about and that's when things began to get difficult. Being such a calculated person, I aim to live my life knowing that every decision I make is for a reason, and I will never say something unless I mean it, or feel it, in that exact moment. And I found it difficult to say that word with feeling. Don't get me wrong, I loved her like a best friend, of that much I am very sure. She knew everything about me – and I, her. We shared everything with each other, hopes, dreams, worries, and we were even each other's 'firsts'. But when I tried to search for something more within myself, I couldn't, and this left me feeling like an imposter.

The fact I couldn't feel anything more beyond what I did, no matter how hard I tried, really started to confuse me and made me feel different to every other couple I would see around me. I mean, guys should really love their girlfriends after a certain amount of time; it just happens, doesn't it? Was I broken? Was I so screwed up from my environment that I was incapable of feeling something 'more' for someone? These were the thoughts I began to have, and the feelings that began to weigh on me. Heavily.

Like I said, hindsight is a great thing, because as I look back on it all now, I think physical chemistry and a strong affinity for each other is what kept things going, and fundamentally, we were different types of people. To this day, I still arrive back to this conclusion, no matter how much contemplation

I give it, because at the end of the day, chemistry is chemistry. Since then, after much thought, I have realised that I find myself only really being able to form physical relationships with women, but the emotional connections fall truly with men. Having learned from life experiences to date, I now recognise relationships and emotions are very complex things, and you can't just force yourself to feel something for someone if you don't already feel that way – it's only natural. This is a very important lesson people need to learn when left wandering the shores of the Land of the Lost Boys, as they risk spending a lifetime waiting to be found.

When things finally came to an end with Her, there was no weight lifted, there was no sense that I was finished playing a role, there was only sadness and a feeling more than ever that I was once again a Lost Boy. As the curtains closed on our relationship her final words remained in my head as she said, 'I need to try something new,' and over the next few months, they were the words I lived by. Whether it was out of some sort of sadness or spite, I felt like I, too, needed to try something new and that I needed to push my boundaries in order to prove I wasn't afraid to try new things; and boy, did I. What ensued next was nothing short of a rollercoaster, full of ups and downs and outright disasters.

It began with Tinder. God bless such a calamitous dating app. Full of judgement, anxiety, dismay and superficiality, but also a godsend for someone looking to 'test the waters' while remaining anonymous. My faceless profile swiped through the surrounding gay and bi male population, bringing with it an anxiety and excitement, similar to what one would feel before going on a first date. Knowing that I was doing something so uncharacteristic to the idealised macho self-image I had of myself was thrilling. I almost felt like a badass, living a double life, as I portrayed myself in one way to the physical world, all the while living in anonymity and letting another side of myself loose in the digital world. It was *almost* liberating.

I must note, while nostalgia clouds my memories like the perfect filter on a below-average photo, I look back on this time as a 'double agent' with fondness, as the idea of having a more-than-meets-the-eye persona is exciting. But in reality, there were a lot of times where loneliness, anxiety and panic surrounded me, as this new side of me flourished like a rare flower; starved of sunlight.

Through Tinder, I was able to find myself amongst a band of Lost Boys. The first guy I ever opened up to from the app was a young sailor of similar age. We talked and talked, and with every message I grew excited for another reply, even eventually swapping numbers. I remember how messaging someone and letting this hidden side of myself run free was so exhilarating and foreign. Then one day he asked me to 'hang out' and grab a coffee. Of course, it had to be in the city, far away from my hometown where I couldn't risk people seeing me. I had never felt so sick with nerves in my life as the train approached the station. I expected some big reveal as I waited for him to step off the platform and through the big sliding glass doors into the sub-zero temperatures of the stone-built terminal to meet me. And there he was, followed by the migration of butterflies in my stomach. 'Wow, you're tall,' were his first words – were the first words from the first guy who was seeing me in this way. And me? Well, my mouth was drier than the desert.

Our second date consisted of much the same, except this time we walked along the lower paths of a semi-secluded trail, alongside a river. It was a heavy summer day, and the sun trickled through the oak leaves in the canopies overhead. The smell of foliage hung in the air and we talked as we walked, and soon the conversation lulled. Gently, a silence fell, louder than anything else. He stood closer while still facing the river, I leaned on the railings and focused on the rushing water as my pulse thumped in my ear. My heart was beating and I was feeling unsteady; I knew something was happening and that's when he leaned in and I experienced my first kiss with another man. I nearly passed out with the shock. Surely this wasn't me; I'm not the guy you would expect to see kissing other guys. My mind turned and body felt weak as I began to give in to these primal urges I was feeling.

Things with the sailor really took a turn for the worse after that, as they tend to with most 'dating' experiences. I guess he got what he wanted, but I'll never forget the rush. The feeling of electricity from that first kiss, the blood coursing through my veins, the softness of another man's lips (which I naïvely expected to be rough and 'manly') and amongst the confusion, I knew it had to mean something. I was starting to build a home in the Land of the Lost Boys, but it was missing something; the feeling of safety from a secret shared.

Speaking your truth can be the hardest thing you ever have to do, but nonetheless, saying it is the most courageous thing you can ever do and it is your defining moment. Upon reflection, our lives are full of moments; some are so ingrained into your being that you'll remember them just as they happened. Others will find you when you least expect it in the form of a sight, sound, or smell which takes you back somewhere you forgot existed. In life, you get rare moments of insight where you just know whatever is about to unfold is one of those moments you will never forget – and in saying those words, you are gifted with a life-long moment. The interesting thing about this particular moment is that it's a common one shared by all those who consider themselves Lost Boys. It's the cement on which the LGBTQ+ community is built, it is the common struggle, and it is the moment where you choose to be brave. Even if you aren't 'out', or you struggle with it, it's a moment/feeling that was, and is, shared by many. It's why the LGBTQ+ community is such a great one to be a part of. It is a worldwide representation of those stood tall in the face of adversity, stood against the beliefs and expectations of not just society, but those who they loved, in order to live their truth; and that's something worth being a part of.

Fast forward a few months since that first kiss and I stood in a crowded kitchen surrounded by older people drinking and having a good time. Music blared as smoke creeped through the air, and I shuffled nervously on the spot, tugging at my denim jacket and building up the courage to have my moment. Sliding through the crowd, I tapped my best friend's arm as she stood at the back door smoking a cigarette. She was veiled in a cloud of smoke that churned under the porch light and discussing college with a boy while gazing into space. 'I need to talk to you, it's really important,' I said. 'Okay, but do I need to put on the kettle? Like, this sounds serious,' she replied playfully, while holding a can of cider.

We walked into the backroom, holding tea-cups filled with alcohol to simulate the sacred intimacy of 'tea and chats'. 'I went on a date with someone,' I started nervously. 'Oh my god, who? *Are you in a relationship and you didn't tell me!*' she screamed, while I knew what was coming next: 'Ehm, no, it was… ehm, with… a guy. And we kissed.' That was it. Those stifled words were my moment (granted, you create many more depending on who it is you are telling). It was my first time saying those words to someone from my 'real life'. From that point on, my fate was sealed and this was the path I was choosing to create, with the goal of finding my way home to myself. She just hugged me and told me how happy she was for me, it was no big deal – and thus marked the start of my journey navigating my way through the Land of the Lost Boys.

As I said, this story is one I will continue to write till the day I die. To date, in my 22 years, it has been filled with so much love and acceptance, and its fair share of heartbreak – but it's worth it. I have by no means left the Land of the Lost Boys behind; at times I find myself alone on the deserted shores and looking for help, while other times I'm partying with the locals and cosying up by the camp fire.

What I hope you take from this is that finding your way through the Land doesn't have to be a lonely journey. While it is a personal one, you don't have to have it all figured out. Only a few short years on, and I still don't know who or what I am – and that's okay. Gay? Bi? To me, right now, they are only labels. What matters is how you feel in navigating your journey and finding ways to make sure it isn't a solo one.

So friend, here we are – immortalised on these pages are the words of my story for all to see. I hope it may help you in finding your way. So here's to you, us, and here's to the Lost Boys (and everyone else) that are just waiting to be found; here's to those who call this Land 'Home'.

Love Always,

Lost Boy.

'CAN'T TURN OFF WHAT TURNS ME ON'

St. Vincent and the masseduction of bisexual style

by a Certified Fan

BISEXUALS HAVE A fashion stereotype, just like everyone else. For us, it probably starts with 'Are you a leather jacket bisexual or a denim jacket bisexual?' It's the famous bi bob; enamel pins on lapels; folding up your jean cuffs; brightly dyed hair. While this stereotype is probably a more accurate descriptor of me than most other stereotypes out there, it's a massively oversimplified way to describe any complex human being and it's far from how I see myself.

Something about the queer world that surprised me (when I found it next to Narnia at the back of the closet) was that it boxes people into these expectations and stereotypes in much the same way that hetero societal pressures do. One might expect that after coming out, the story ends with either freedom and happiness or, at the other extreme, devastation and ruin; not so, for most. Life's challenges, social expectations and little joys go on. In between it all, queers see the same photoshopped celebrities on magazine covers that everyone else sees. We all live under capitalism and patriarchy together. We order too much on ASOS to find our true selves in the mirror, just like straight people do.

I'm a strong believer that each individual should express their identity however they wish, and for many, I'd hope this takes the form of something deeper than simple aesthetics and fabrics. Me, though – I always need to start by making it visual, and if I could visually embody my identity, I'd become St. Vincent.

When I say St. Vincent I hope you understand I mean the bisexual singer-songwriter and record producer Annie Clark, who goes by that stage name. I obviously do not mean St. Vincent the Deacon of Saragossa. I know nothing about him and if you've picked up the wrong Bible, then this essay out of all of them is probably not the one for you.

I first came across St. Vincent while at uni, when I heard she was coming to town and I decided to try to make myself love her enough to justify buying a ticket (not a lot of performers came to my city back then... nor do they now, really). I convinced myself fully that she was worth the expense and my excitement built steadily, but when pay day came, tickets had sold out. I listened to 'Digital Witness' all night and felt sorry for myself, sitting at home with the cat, while Annie was probably riffing up a storm in the city's one appropriate venue. From there, she became part of a goal of mine somehow. To see her live at a time when I was more me; when I'd worked out where life was going; to know her music better alongside knowing myself better; next time...

This essay is about my sexuality, so you're probably expecting me to make a grand confession that St. Vincent is my devastatingly unattainable crush – the celeb love of my life that I'll never meet – but she's not. I see parts of myself in her and her music and her videos; or at least, I want to. I see a public figure I relate to and strive to be like, just like straight women have whoever they have and lesbians have

Cate Blanchett. (Though if St. Vincent is to me what Cate Blanchett is to lesbians, maybe it is some sort of meta crush after all…? You tell me.)

One thing that's been important to me when processing my bisexuality while listening to St. Vincent's music is that St. Vincent makes me feel *cool*. There are sad queer songs everywhere out there; we can sob our guts out to Troye Sivan's 'Heaven' and often need to. Likewise, there are gay bar bangers like 'YMCA' that…don't even get me started on that side of things, actually. Somewhere outside all that 'Pride month on the radio' stuff, there's me listening to 'Cruel' or 'The Strangers'. Not feeling a part of any 'community', not feeling excluded from any 'society'; just feeling like myself in my old box room at my parents' house. The moment that smells and sounds like home, rain on the window in the background (likely), tea in hand with a cat hair in it (definitely), sitting on the floor because there is no seat, playing a song by my favourite singer. *Feeling cool.* Feeling something big in my chest; calm acceptance. Security. Also experiencing a deeply appealing sense of style. A way to keep that feeling with me is clothes; is music gigs; is records; posters; keeping my earphones in while walking through a world that's sometimes not mine.

It's going to sound lame to say it, but we get enough negativity sent to Queer Central; St. Vincent has often just made gal love just look so aspirational, strong, beautiful and desirable. She's had a very public (sadly now defunct) relationship with Cara Delevigne, and her album *Masseduction* is allegedly a love letter and eulogy to their relationship. She stands by her admiration of her ex-girlfriend when she sings her into a 'hero' and 'friend' for whom she'd 'do it all again'. I can't help but think that kind of healthy respect, especially when woman to woman, is awe-inspiring. Perhaps also notable here is that St. Vincent also dated the girl from *Twilight* whose name escapes me, but I realise now I don't have much to say on that, except they both wore sunglasses at lot during that period – which perhaps implies their experiences of bi-erasure somehow.

St. Vincent isn't shallow, though, that's not what I'm saying. Her music is loaded with genius, weirdness, emotions, beauty and sometimes hurt. Her performances are artworks in themselves, with concept video installations, guitars she makes especially for women's bodies and fist punches into the air sending love to all the 'freaks'. She uses her platform to advocate for what she believes in and is public about her politics; supporting Planned Parenthood, holding hands with female partners at London Fashion Week, denouncing conservatism. She's liberal in every way; to me, I see her and I see art and truth. She backs up the performance, I guess is what I'm saying. I like to think that I do too. Or that I'll try to, every time there's another 'next time'…

This year, Annie performed an edgy, Sapphic rendition of 'Masseduction' x 'One Kiss' with Dua Lipa at the Grammys. Annie clad in all black and signature thick velvet choker, Dua Lipa at her shoulder in black and white, performing a tense empowering duet with matching bi bobs under acoustic lighting. I'm sold. It's good for me to be sold. It's a good thing for me to recognise that I admire this kind of queer female performance, because my attraction is still mostly geared towards men. It's at odds with this that I've found myself spending life with a female partner (my own personal 'only motherfucker in the city who can stand me'), and when that all began, I found it bizarre to think that people would now see me as part of a same sex pairing.

This leads me to recall the first time I saw two women kiss; it was also on stage. A TV stage, Eurovision, and it was t.A.T.u. I asked my mom why girls would kiss one another and she said 'Some people are lesbians' and I took that to mean the same kind of thing as 'Some people are Italian'. Maybe I thought lesbian was a nationality. I checked my passport in my head that night and I was still Irish, so I guess I ignored one part of my sexuality for quite a few years after that. Stage performances still stand out to me though, perhaps because I'm not much one for getting up in front of others like that, making it all the more impressive to me when I see love or queerness put out there in the way Annie Clark does it (and she does it in thigh-high latex stilettos too; I stan a bold queen).

I finally saw St. Vincent live in 2018, in London, under a blazing sun. Everything smelled like new summer grass, felt like a distant onslaught of hayfever, and tasted like £8.50 gin and tonic. I was wearing black and white stripy trousers and I can't remember what my girlfriend wore, but I'm sure she looked cute too, as per the theme of my fashionable essay and her own parallel cute, fashionable life. Annie shouted 'Girls! Boys!' to open 'Sugarboy' (must be because she likes both too!) and I felt like we'd found our crowd, holding hands tight so as not to lose each other while trying to sneak our way to the front. Holding hands tight as I wanted to stay rooted in that feeling and to anchor my truth to my girlfriend too; acceptance. Security. Also experiencing a deeply appealing sense of style. I saw St. Vincent again later in 2018, with an old friend, and during a fight with my girlfriend after we'd just moved in together. Annie sang 'New York' and I knew who I loved, regardless of arguments.

Maybe it seems materialistic to centre this piece around a singer and her style, but if I can't show it then you can't see me, right? There's something about creativity that uncovers the greatest beauty and strength in humanity, in my opinion. St. Vincent explores materialism quite a bit in her lyrics and videos, namely in 'Los Ageless' and 'Digital Witness'. In

'Los Ageless' she parodies the many rigid vanity rituals we go through, and shows how science fiction-esque these start to look if we even just flip the familiar colour palette for a second. In 'Digital Witness' she looks at the TV and thinks it might as well just be a window, she's seeing so much of the same thing.

Her song 'Pills', which admittedly took me longer to warm up to than most of her work, is about how people often numb their way through the rat race. Its tune sounds like the jingle in a cheap American commercial and draws attention to the damage creepy 21st-century lifestyles are having on us. It's not anti-medication, as I initially thought. In a YouTube interview she stated that her ex Cara Delevigne features as a background vocalist on the track because facing mental ill-health together was something that bonded them during their relationship, and the song was in part them laughing at themselves as well as processing what they've been through. Her track 'Young Lover' relates to this too, as it centres worrying about a lover's wellbeing. While in many tracks, especially the newer ones, she processes difficult things (such as in 'Severed Crossed Fingers' where on surface level she seems to throw away hope altogether), there always seems to be so much more to St. Vincent to combat any sense of sadness; I see a keen enthusiasm to create more, to pour more blue paint over her face, to stand under an umbrella in a flower shop, to try all the weird and wonderful things life has to offer. This energy transfers to me as someone who often struggles with life's pressures.

In putting this essay together, I've realised more than ever the need we have not just for perfect queer 'role models' but just to shake up the familiar, stagnant system entirely. Annie Clark shakes up the system; she paints New York pastel purple and vivid red, she writes NO on orange paper and she puts it through a shredder. I want to stop seeing the same photoshopped faces everywhere; I want to stop seeing Primark making cheap versions of the stock in all the other high street clothes shops because it's a given that people will all buy the same stuff if they're told that's how to look.

If you came to this essay hoping I could help you with some profound revelations about life, well, then just like St. V, 'honey, I can't be your saviour'. But I can encourage you to find a song or album that makes you feel just like yourself. Don't worry about coming out or queerphobia (even just for a second). Don't worry about that person who doesn't love you back or who laughed at your excess of leopard print. Put on that magenta pink vinyl and inhale those stylish good vibes; I hope you feel how *cool* it can be to just be queer and alive. And maybe we'll dance in the same crowd someday, dressed up, worry-free and belting out 'Fast Slow Disco'.

HOW LOUISA MAY ALCOTT HELPED ME TO SURVIVE BEING OUTED

by Jo Landon

BEING AN EVANGELICAL bookworm, I have always tried to rationalise the world around me through literature. I also looked for versions of myself in the pages of my favourite novels. Like many 'tomboys' I found my literary soulmate in Little Women's Jo March. Reading the description of Jo in that opening chapter was like coming home:

> 'Fifteen-year-old Jo was very tall, thin, and brown, and reminded one of a colt, for she never seemed to know what to do with her long limbs, which were very much in her way. She had a decided mouth, a comical nose, and sharp, gray eyes, which appeared to see everything, and were by turns fierce, funny, or thoughtful. Her long, thick hair was her one beauty, but it was usually bundled into a net, to be out of her way. Round shoulders had Jo, big hands and feet, a flyaway look to her clothes, and the uncomfortable appearance of a girl who was rapidly shooting up into a woman and didn't like it.'[1]

These lines paint a picture for the reader, but also turn a key in the hearts of those of us who find ourselves in Jo. Her lack of interest in vanity, her creative energy built up like a spinning top about to take off in any direction, and her unwillingness to settle for the gendered customs of the time speak to any girl or woman who has felt trapped and dreamt of something more for herself. It's rare and refreshing to find physical descriptions of a young woman as 'decided,' 'comical,' 'sharp,' 'flyaway' and 'uncomfortable,' especially when such characteristics are maintained and celebrated throughout the four-book series rather than gradually chastened and removed.

I desperately held out hope that Jo would defy Victorian tradition and remain single, until my hopes were dashed at the end of *Good Wives*[2] when she settles for Professor Bhaer. I was at least pleased that her male suitor was chosen based on a meeting of minds over anything else. Reading on in *Little Men*[3] and *Jo's Boys*[4], I was heartened to find Jo as independent as ever despite the trappings of wedlock, never overshadowed by her husband. I was relieved to discover that Alcott was as disappointed as I was to be forced by her publisher to give her alter ego the 'happy ending' of marriage.

I also admired Alcott's work ethic; she trained herself to write with her left hand so that her ambidexterity would lead to longer hours at her writing desk. She bestowed this ambition on her protagonist. I can't help but imagine this ambidexterity as symbolic of the androgyny and bisexual undertones that I perceive when reading Alcott's work.

My bi-rometer bleeps whenever I make my annual revisit to the March family saga. Years after my first reading and while researching the biography of Alcott for some lectures I delivered in a university module on 19th-Century Literature, my bi-rometric alerts were further amplified by a quotation from an interview that Alcott gave. In response to a question about why she never married, Alcott states, 'I am more than half-persuaded that I am a man's soul put by some freak of nature into a woman's body... because I have fallen in love with so many pretty girls and never once the least bit with any man' (Showalter)[4]. One could speculate that there are allusions to a trans identity. I also see this (perhaps even cling to it) as potential evidence of Alcott's bisexuality.[*]

There is more bi representation in literature and pop culture now, so I no longer need to go searching for, or indeed, imagine it. For example, the protagonist of one of my favourite TV shows, *Legends of Tomorrow*[6], is a bisexual time-travelling woman[**]. However, in my teenage years I had to use a mixture of imagination and detective skills to seek out potential bi role models. The solace I found in literature became all the more important when my secondary school principal outed me to my parents without my knowledge or permission. He informed them that their 'daughter is a homosexual', completely erasing my bi identity and utterly shattering the thin ice that divided my surface relationship with my parents from who I really am. The conditions my parents placed on their love sliced through me with a savagery that can only be driven by the velocity of hatred, insecurity and fear: cold warnings about what would happen if this revelation ever became public, statements of what should be done 'to correct faggots and fanny lickers', and a permanent frost of shame and revulsion. From that day on I slept with my bedroom door locked and a screwdriver under my mattress.

They considered sending me away to boarding school, and in that moment I was reminded of a common threat that was made during my childhood: 'Be good or I'll send you to

---

[*] *Showalter also perceives this statement as evidence of bisexuality expressed with the 'candid innocence of a pre-Freudian' (xx).*

[**] *Sara Lance is played by Caity Lotz. The character also appears in DC's TV show, Arrow.*

Bessborough.'*** As a child Bessborough sounded like something caught in my throat. It made my eyes water. My chest tightened and I tried to purge myself of Adam's rib caught behind my tonsils. As a teenager I learned that Bessborough was once a home for 'bad girls' and 'fallen women.' I was lucky that these hellholes no longer operated at the time that I was outed. The last Magdalene Laundry had been shut down only eight years before. I still shudder when I think about what particular brand of Catholic punishment would have awaited me if the church were still policing women and girls as heavily as they once had. It's a typical Irish approach to a 'problem': send it away, hide it, ignore it, and don't talk about it.

These particular places were primarily used to imprison, enslave and torture women and girls who became pregnant outside of marriage: 'promiscuous' women, women with impaired mental development, criminals, orphans, women living in poverty, or women deemed to be generally immoral for any reason. Ireland has a long history of locking away those who are deemed in any way beyond the confines of what's acceptable. There's a long-whispered story in my family about a distant cousin who was raped in her early teens, and then repeatedly incarcerated in an asylum by the local priest every time she had an emotional breakdown because of her trauma.

My parents were of that particularly repressed ilk of Irish Catholics who deferred to the church and other authority figures in the community. When I was but four years old my mother took me to the doctor and, after informing him that I preferred to play with boys' toys, asked, 'What's wrong with her?' Even now, I am grateful to that doctor for assuring her that it was only normal for a little girl in a house full

---

*** Bessborough was a Mother and Baby home located in Co Cork, Ireland.

of brothers to want to share their toys. I know now that my mother's worries were almost certainly about what she saw as the threat of homosexuality, which was still a criminal offence in Ireland at the time. So many parents of my LGBTQ+ friends have told me that they knew from when their child was a young age that they were not straight. I'm sure my mother knew too. I dread to think of what kind of corrective treatment could have been prescribed by a more cloistered doctor.

The school principal informed my parents that my ambitions to be a teacher would never come to pass because 'no school would hire a homosexual.' Indeed this is true; up to 2015, Ireland's Employment Equality Act that protects workers from discrimination included a loophole that allowed religious institutions like schools and hospitals to discriminate against people who did not fit with their 'ethos.' Even as a student I was discriminated against in the name of my school's Catholic ethos. The day after the school principal spoke to my parents, I sobbed in his office and implored him to explain why he did this to me. I was given a speech about the Catholic ethos of the school, and his 'duty of care to the other students.' The latter took the wind out of me. The insinuation was that I was somehow dangerous when at that very moment I was terrified for my own safety both in my school and under my own roof.

I have moved through life broken by the knowledge that my parents will only care for a false version of me, a waxen doll sculpted from their icy vision of frigid, straight, docile Irish girlhood. At the time that I was outed, we were studying the poetry of Eavan Boland. I was particularly struck by 'The Shadow Doll'[7], especially the lines about being 'Under glass, under wraps' (142). The lines capture the repression that surrounded me in rural Ireland, a fog so thick it seemed to almost clog my pores, plug my airways, and cloud the reality that there was more out there for me than my then situation. It seems to me that Boland's 'The Shadow Doll' is a quintessential poem about Irish girlhood. She uses the Victorian doll, given to brides-to-be by dressmakers to model their wedding dresses, as a metaphor for how marriage transforms a woman into a 'porcelain bride in an airless glamour' (142), vacuum-packed in the gendered expectations of wifehood. While Boland's poem is about the constraints that traditional heterosexual marriage can place on women in their private and public roles, it speaks to me of the many other ways in which womanhood is forced to cleave to heteronormativity.

As a teenager, my metaphorical shadow doll was hauled out of the closet just long enough to make me feel ashamed of its existence and fearful for my personal safety. Just like the 'battered tan case' (142) in 'The Shadow Doll', my parents and the school principal 'pressing down, then pressing down again, then locks' (142) with their words and gestures, shutting me in and away, forced to become a blind spot in their Catholic culture.

Boland's wedding gifts of 'coffee pots and clocks' (142) remind her of the domestic expectations of a wife, and the lifelong commitment assumed in the act of getting married. I wonder, if my outing came with gifts, what I would have been given. Perhaps a chastity belt given that my parents – like so many ignorant homophobes – associate queerness with 'deviance' and hypersexuality. Although, given their fixation with Irish Catholic solutions to Irish Catholic problems, I suspect I would have been presented with a one-way ticket to a church-run institution had those still been in existence.

While my parents and school colluded to reduce me to a vanishing point in their world, I found a small community, two LGBTQ+ friends to confide in and feel a sense of connection that I had never experienced before outside of literature and pop culture. I grew up in a place that you might refer to as a local town for local people, as you may have guessed given the actions of the school principal. Everyone knew everyone else's business and you either lived by certain heteronormative codes or you were shunned and labelled one of the village weirdos. It's the kind of village where everyone in the local pub will turn and stare when a 'blow in' crosses the threshold.

Even as a young child falling in love with Sinead O'Connor when I first saw her, bald and beautiful, in the 'Nothing Compares 2 U'[8] video, I knew not to voice my feelings, especially when my parents would sneer at the television and say 'she's not a real woman.' I did, however, declare that I would one day shave my head just like O'Connor's, much to my mother's horror. Even though I didn't learn the word 'bisexual' until I was about 14 years of age, I understood that my identity did not fit with the future that was already constructed for me from birth. Short hair, tattoos, muscular bodies, outspokenness and queerness were all considered unladylike. When I voiced my desire, as a teenager, to attend university my ambitions were met with my mother's response to, 'wait until you get out of nappies.'

Artists are attracted to where I grew up by the light that frames sublime landscapes for them to paint and sketch. Its darker corners and alleys are overcast with a longstanding suspicion of anything that isn't white, straight and Catholic. It's an easier place to live now if you are someone whose selfhood exists outside the confines of 'normal.' But before Irish marriage equality, pre-Panti Bliss's speech at the Abbey Theatre, pre-openly gay politicians, it was stifling. I survived by hiding in those very shadows. There's no shame in it. If it's not safe to be out, then we need to care for ourselves first. I was forced out into an unsafe situation. I had to deny that part of myself to keep a roof over my head and ensure that my body and mind were as protected as they could possibly be. When my father attempted to strangle me a week after my 18th birthday I saw a world of hatred and disgust cycloning in his mad eyes. I was not the daughter he wanted.

I identify so much with Jo March in the chapter where her sisters groan over her shorn hair that she sells to raise money for Marmee's journey to care for their father. My mother clung to my thick white blond hair as the one symbol of my straight girlhood. Every last hair follicle brought me nothing but dismay and anxiety until I had it cut short when I was 17 years old, not long after my school principal outed me. Not only did it stand for the suffocation of heteronormativity, it seemed to be some sort of beacon that attracted unwanted hands running through it, unnecessary and inappropriate comments about the hearts that I would someday break. Each lock of hair fell to the salon floor like bars coming away from a prison cell. My mother wept when she saw my new hairdo. She was more visibly upset by my shorn locks than by my trauma at being outed against my will. It's a harsh realisation that one of your body parts is more valued than your personhood by the people who are supposed to love you unconditionally.

Beginning with the haircut, I began a slow process of taking ownership of my body as a means of healing my mind. Most recently, I had a pin-up of Jo March tattooed on my forearm.**** She is standing by her writing desk with her short hair and inky fingers, clutching her manuscript, looking determined, creative and independent, just like that initial description of her in the opening pages of Little Women. The tattoo, another one of my parents' markers of unladylike

---

**** Very special thanks to Alexandra Wilkey for designing and tattooing my March pin-up.

behaviour, is a permanent reminder to me that I am a person of my own making, that I have a right to be my authentic self, and not anyone else's false image. Just as Boland's 'Shadow Doll' 'survives its occasion' I survive mine and keep bodily reminders of my freedom. In the tattoo, both of Jo's hands are ink-stained, a reminder of Alcott's ambidexterity. Literary critic Elaine Showalter sees Alcott's writerly ambidexterity as a 'metaphor for her creativity' both under her own name and under her pseudonym***** which she switched between for different audiences and literary styles (ix). I had to be ambidextrous in my own way, hiding in the shadows of my home's and school's compulsory heterosexuality for safety's sake, while finding ways to preserve my selfhood in my body and mind. I'm now at a point in my life where I exist proudly beyond the shadows. But there are still times when I have to retreat, and I think it's important to remember that this is a necessary act of self-preservation sometimes.

Despite my school principal's belief that I would never work as a teacher, I now work as a university lecturer. I've had the privilege of working in Ireland at a time when we achieved marriage equality, abortion rights, and the gender recognition act. I have seen students' attitudes and self-expression evolve and be increasingly celebrated. To channel Alcott, they are truly 'sailing [their] own ships.' But I have also had many conversations with students who have come to me for support as an LGBTQ+ lecturer, still in fear of conservative parents, still worried that their sexual orientation or gender identity will impact on their career ambitions.

Just like Alcott switched her quill from one hand to another, some of us have to move through the world in a state of flux, and just like Alcott's ability made her a more

_____
***** Alcott wrote sensational stories under the pseudonym, A. M. Barnard.

productive writer, I believe this flexibility makes me and my bi comrades stronger. I still hold my identity in my heart and wear it on my skin even when I have to hold that part of myself in. I would be a rather disappointing bisexual word-smith if I were not to note the B and I in ambidextrous. What I admire most about bisexuals is our flexibility, not just in terms of who we love, but how we survive. Perhaps another word for bisexual is am-bi-dextrous.

A MAN, A CANE, AN AWKWARD TITLE

Adventures of a bisexual, disabled, genderqueer writer

by Sandra Alland

WRITING THIS AT 45 years old, I started to question whether I've focused enough on my bisexuality in the 20 years I've been publishing poems, stories and arts journalism. If almost no one seems to know this thing about me – it must be my fault, right?

I grew up in Scarborough, outside Taranton/T'karonto (aka Toronto), in a white settler, working-class-striving-for-middle-class family. I was raised by my Dutch/French-Canadian mother, and Scottish-migrant grandfather and father. Though my parents indulged my love of Boy George, they never imagined I wanted to be him. I had boyfriends and girlfriends from when I was young, but quickly learned not to talk about the girlfriends or the times I 'pretended' I was a boy (who was sometimes also a girl). It was the 1980s and I lived in a small community; I didn't find words for what I lived or felt.

When I left high school in 1992, neither George Michael nor my two gay teachers felt safe enough to be out. But I did come out, sort of, at 19. I was three years into a six-year relationship with a broke Yugoslavian-Canadian, helping him raise his little brother in a Toronto flat we couldn't afford. I came out quietly – while I was working two jobs, trying to be the first person in my family to go to university, and dealing with PTSD from childhood sexual abuse. While my boyfriend became addicted to drugs. While I endured daily migraines and chronic pain that meant I couldn't pick up a pen. We nodded tiredly to my sexuality as we waded through the growing piles of trauma and complexity we had no space for – including the possibility of his bisexuality, too. We loved each other messily and hard.

I didn't know anyone queer, and I was distinctly un-Toronto, un-middle-class and un-well. So I wrote in the brief moments I found while commuting to work. I wrote to stay alive.

Several years and partners later, my thin chapbook of poems, The Mathematics of Love, was published by a tiny press (Thirteenth Tiger). It became my coming-out card for the new millennium; I handed it to folk, including my parents, rather than having 'that talk' (again). I remember my boss running into my box-office cubicle after reading it and shouting, 'I didn't know you were bisexual!' Like I had somehow betrayed him by not including it on my CV. (Here's something *I* didn't know, Rick. There was a carbon monoxide leak in the theatre that probably wasn't great for my already-shite health).

My band in the late 1990s, Stumblin' Tongues, also featured my poems about bi love and loss. As did my first full-length book, Proof of a Tongue. When it was published in 2004, most of Toronto's cis and straight literary people weren't interested in LGBTQI+ poems (not sure if they are yet), and most gay and lesbian writers ignored bisexuals. Luckily for me, a few people saw me read around town, people who didn't focus on Gold Star Lesbianism and biological determinism.

I waited until I was 31 to publish my first book, but even that happened mostly by fluke (mixed with white privilege). A young queer writer, Zoe Whittall, fished my manuscript out of a tall stack of submissions at McGilligan Books. If it weren't for the attention of a stranger, I might still be waiting – as many people are. Especially those who aren't white, or can't drag themselves up 43 stairs to a poetry reading.

Over the years, I also published poems in *Anything That Moves*, San Francisco's now-defunct bisexual magazine, and Toronto's *Fence Magazine*. I wrote articles clarifying I wasn't a lesbian or a woman. I created flawed but innovative poetry-theatre pieces about my fluid sexuality and gender at Toronto's Theatre Centre and Buddies in Bad Times Theatre. So why was my name still showing up in 'lesbian literary round-ups'?

This was over 12 years ago, before the internet was as much of a thing for most people. So maybe my reach just wasn't that far. Reviewers called my bisexual book a lesbian book, and it stuck. They assumed the poems about men were from before I came out, which was assumed to be 'now'. Maybe I needed to say it again?

But here's where harmful behaviour from many 'LGBT' organisations comes into play. I couldn't submit my book to Canada's Lesbian and Gay Archives – unless I wanted to be both misgendered and erased as bi. And *Proof of a Tongue* was published fourteen years before Lambda recognised 'bisexual poetry' as a literary award category (in 2018!). The 'b' was *very* silent back then.

To be totally honest, I did briefly give up and let myself 'gay-pass'. I was certainly being discriminated against like a lesbian, so maybe the distinction that I was a genderqueer bisexual pansy wasn't so important? I also felt it might be more vital to focus on heterosexual privilege, because it seemed maybe some bisexuals (including me) sometimes benefitted from something like it.

The less I corrected assumptions, the more I was welcomed (and hired) by the lesbian and gay community. But the idea of 'privilege' faded as I learned how it's falsely weaponised against bi people. Nobody gets a job or flat over somebody else by declaring their bisexuality. Truth is, we experience higher rates of sexual and domestic violence, poverty, homelessness and mental ill-health than gay men and lesbians.

I began to insist, again, on 'queer' or 'bisexual'; 'lesbian' erased not only me, but also some of my partners. People urged me to 'just come out' – when I already had, over and over. I realised acceptance rested on my complicity in my own oppression, and that of other bi (and trans) people.

Work dwindled. Bad mental health knocked on my door, repeatedly.

I'm alive because I finally found a community of LGBTQI+ co-conspirators who didn't do bullshit. I'm grateful to the writers and artists, many of them BIPOC (Black, Indigenous and/or people of colour), who taught me much and had patience with my failings. To the radical innovators of that often-magical time, like Karen Miranda Augustine, Spy Dénommé-Welch, Trish Salah, Anna Camilleri, Naila Keleta Mae, Nathanaël Stephens, Tara-Michelle Ziniuk, Riley Skelton, d'bi.young anitafrika, Corrina Hodgson and Leah Lakshmi Piepzna-Samarasinha. And I'll never forget the group of cis-het poets attending a workshop I organised at This Ain't The Rosedale Library bookshop – who used the pronoun 'they' for my lover, without questioning. I'll never forget the bravery of that lover.

We all wrote our way back alive in rare and liminal spaces, in the margins of everything (not) said about us. I fucked up, fell down, smoked and drank too much. But because I wrote, and because I had my people, finally, I didn't disappear.

When I moved to Edinburgh in 2007, hardly anyone used the words 'queer' or 'trans' – and many gay events were unwelcoming to me and the brilliant migrant, Latinx, Black, Polish, disabled, D/deaf and/or skint people I began to collaborate with. I started a queer and trans reading series, Who's Your Dandy?, and then in 2009 a group of us founded the queer and trans arts project, Cachín Cachán Cachunga!

With growing unease, I noted the UK (white, middle-class) feminist tendency towards SWERFism and TERFism. I was thrilled to find positive takes on sex work in articles by a local writer called Nine. But sex workers and trans people were still derided by many English and Scottish 'feminists'. I met my first Sex-Worker/Trans Exclusionary Radical Feminist in the supposed safety of a now-defunct feminist/radical bookshop where I worked, when they enthusiastically hosted a talk by Sheila Jeffreys.

My jaw dropped when I read a *Guardian* article by another SWERF/TERF, Julie Bindel, defining queer as 'kinky sex'. She also used this national platform to claim trans people silenced her, and to ridicule androgyny and bisexuality as 'odd sexual habits' analogous to 'cat-fancying' and 'devil-worshipping'. I shook when a poet I later shared a stage with asked if 'queer' meant I had sex with animals.

As time passed, I watched as 'queer' overcame these assaults, but also lost its North American meaning of fighting pinkwashing, homonationalism, and rigid gender and sexual binaries... to become a white, British, middle-class synonym for 'gay and lesbian'.

I was suddenly not bisexual, again.

When queer events popped up more regularly in Scotland, I listened as cis gay folk said 'trans' for a bit, then stopped saying it, because queer meant that too now (only it didn't, because there were still no trans people running things). I watched as gay pubs said, 'No trainers or trackies', as places like Polo Lounge refused to let in people of colour and kicked out disabled people (or were too inaccessible for them to get in in the first place). My stomach flipped when LGBT charities collaborated with police services that oppressed our communities. When trans people got arrested at Glasgow Pride. When a trans charity suggested hiring security for an event I organised because it was at Priscilla's, a working-class pub.

And when similar discrimination played out back in Toronto.

I moved to Glasgow, back to Edinburgh, then to Glasgow again. I fell in and out of love. I survived sexual assault (again). I went through the horrors of our court system twice, because of racist and homo/transphobic violence against my loved ones. I experienced violence from a loved one. I got very, very tired.

Meanwhile, constant disclosure gnawed away at my psyche; being permanently 'deceptive' just plain wore me down.

My short hair and black boots mean a lot of folk in Scotland assume I'm lesbian, until I show up with a man on my arm. Then my sexuality gets called into question; it has suddenly changed. I'm assumed cis until I dress certain ways or present particular language: 'they' pronouns or the title 'Mx'.

Similarly, people everywhere assume I'm non-disabled. Even those who know that my art features disabled communities scoff or stare blankly when I ask to take the lift. They declare how good I am for helping 'those people'. But when I use a walking stick or arm-splints, it ends some of the invisibility of chronic pain, fibromyalgia, hypermobility, scoliosis, mental ill-health and cognitive issues. Yet, this ending isn't met with recognition, but instead disbelief or concern: 'What happened to you?' As if suddenly something has changed. Even from people I've told I'm ill for 25 *years*:

'Get better soon!' My brokenness made manifest, yet still impermanent.

A man, a cane, an awkward title – symbols of something not as it should be. Symbols that, when seen, are followed by anger. People have somehow been tricked. I've tricked them; I am the trick. And now they have to make unnecessary effort.

After I had trans-awareness training brought into a theatre where I worked in Edinburgh, a co-worker said: 'Good morning, madame. I mean, sir. I mean, it.' He was sweating and red with the change I'd forced on him, the perceived deception. My discomfort and trauma didn't enter his thoughts.

These tricks work in reverse, too. If someone meets me using a cane and then the next time we meet I don't use it – am I really disabled? If they know me to have a boyfriend, and then I make out with a woman – why didn't I tell them I was gay?

I've changed. I'm always changing. Why have I changed, again, without letting them know? The disbelief in, and erasure of, my bisexual, genderqueer, and invisibly/unevenly-ill personhood knows no bounds. I won't even mention what happens when I say I'm Scottish.

As an organiser, I've spent many years requesting access for disabled, D/deaf and neurodivergent people. There's often outrage when I do this, but especially when those I challenge don't view me as 'really' disabled. If I can walk up stairs sometimes, why am I complaining? If I'm in a relationship with a man, why am I still going on about the need for LGBTQI+ spaces? If most days I can enter the women's toilet without harassment, why is it a big deal what my gender 'really' is? Why should they care if I'm not actually *real*?

I still publish, but after 20 years of readings and performances, I almost never read in public. Not because I'm ill, though that factors in. I avoid events that don't have basic disabled and D/deaf access, are 'women-only', don't pay a fee or at least travel (especially if they charge admission), and/or suck at alphabets (no POC, B, T or I). I didn't read at all in 2018.

Few LGBT or arts organisers ensure wide-ranging (or any) access. Some do the bare minimum for one-off events or festivals, like limited British Sign Language interpreting and spaces you can squeeze a wheelchair into. But usually, instead of improving access when disabled people request it, organisers shame us for costs (or spoiling their party), frame us as 'angry' for asking, or just stop inviting us altogether. So, I do not read.

When women's collectives invite me, I don't usually reply anymore. But sometimes I accept and inform them I'm genderqueer. Despite my experiences of daily misogyny, many are offended I'd 'take up' women's space. (Where's non-binary or agender space?) Sometimes I'm allowed to participate, with caveats. Throughout much of 2018, Glasgow Women's Library stated their women-only events permitted 'non-binary and gender fluid people who identify in a significant way as woman or female'. Though GWL replaced this definition as of 2019, and have strongly stated their solidarity with trans people, other Scottish organisations have already exactly adopted their previous wording. I can occupy space, if I'm okay with a definition anathema to most definitions of non-binary. If I'm okay with being misgendered by everyone in the room. So, I do not read.

But I'm still here, writing. Sometimes dictating each sentence because I can't type. Sometimes lying in bed, writing words in my head because I'm too sore or sad to move. I write for the friends, lovers and family who never erased me. I write for the people I didn't get it right with. I dream of space for those who never leave bed, for those whose visible difference means facing constant danger, and for all artists who are ill, sad, mad, tired, or worn down by racism, classism, ableism, fatism, ageism, cis-heterosexism and bi-erasure. I insist on our presence, our unique histories, the complexity and specificity of each name we choose to give ourselves.

REFERENCES

All the Things She Said

1. Piccalo, Gina. 'Borderline Personality Disorder and Sex.' 2010. Retrieved from https://www.thedailybeast.com/borderline-personality-disorder-and-sex

Erotic Computer

1. Lorde, Audre. *Your Silence Will Not Protect You.* Silver Press, 2017. Print.
2. Spanos, Brittany. 'Janelle Monáe Frees Herself.' *Rolling Stone.* April 26, 2018. https://www.rollingstone.com/music/music-features/janelle-monae-frees-herself-629204/.

'I Still Feel Like I Can't Quite Be Myself'

1. Herek, G. M. (2002). Heterosexuals' attitudes toward bisexual men and women in the United States. *Journal of sex research*, 39(4), 264-274.
2. Yost, M. R., & Thomas, G. D. (2012). Gender and binegativity: Men's and women's attitudes toward male and female bisexuals. *Archives of Sexual Behavior*, 41(3), 691-702.
3. Sarno, E., & Wright, A. J. (2013). Homonegative microaggressions and identity in bisexual men and women. *Journal*

of Bisexuality, 13(1), 63-81.

4. Mitchell, R. C., Davis, K. S., & Galupo, M. P. (2015). Comparing perceived experiences of prejudice among self-identified plurisexual individuals. Psychology & Sexuality, 6(3), 245-257.

5. Mohr, J. J., & Rochlen, A. B. (1999). Measuring attitudes regarding bisexuality in lesbian, gay male, and heterosexual populations. Journal of Counseling Psychology, 46(3), 353.

6. Bradford, M. (2004). The Bisexual Experience: Living in a Dichotomous Culture. Journal of Bisexuality, 4(1–2), 7–23. https://doi.org/10.1300/J159v04n01_02

7. Erickson-Schroth, L., & Mitchell, J. (2009). Queering queer theory, or why bisexuality matters. Journal of Bisexuality, 9(3-4), 297-315.

8. Balsam, K. F., & Mohr, J. J. (2007). Adaptation to sexual orientation stigma: A comparison of bisexual and lesbian/ gay adults. Journal of Counseling Psychology, 54(3), 306.

9. Duca, J. (1991). Needs Assessment of the Bisexual Community. Gay and Lesbian Community Action Council, Minneapolis, Minnesota.

10. Burleson, W. E. (2012). Bisexual Community Needs Assessment. Bisexual Organizing Project, Minneapolis, Minnesota.

11. Rust, P. C. (1995). Bisexuality and the challenge to lesbian politics: Sex, loyalty, and revolution. NYU Press.

12. Pachankis, J. E., & Goldfried, M. R. (2004). Clinical issues in working with lesbian, gay, and bisexual clients. Psychotherapy: Theory, research, practice, training, 41(3), 227.

13. McLean, K. (2008a). Inside, outside, nowhere: Bisexual men and women in the gay and lesbian community. Journal of Bisexuality, 8(1-2), 63-80.

14. Lingel, J. (2009). Adjusting the borders: Bisexual passing and queer theory. Journal of Bisexuality, 9(3-4), 381-405.

15. Udis-Kessler, A. (1995). Identity/politics: A history of the bisexual movement. *Bisexual politics: Theories, queries, and visions*, 17-30.

16. McLean, K. (2008b). Silences and stereotypes: The impact of (mis) constructions of bisexuality on Australian bisexual men and women. *Gay and Lesbian Issues and Psychology Review*, 4(3), 158.

17. Rothblum, E. (2010). Where is the 'women's community? 'Voices of lesbian, bisexual, and queer women and heterosexual sisters. *Feminism & Psychology*, 20(4), 454-472.

18. Crowley, M. S. (2010). Experiences of young bisexual women in lesbian/bisexual groups on MySpace. *Journal of Bisexuality*, 10(4), 388-403.

19. McLean, K. (2001). Living life in the double closet: Bisexual youth speak out. *Hecate*, 27(1), 109.

20. Rankin, S., Weber, G. N., Blumenfeld, W. J., & Frazer, S. (2010). *2010 state of higher education for lesbian, gay, bisexual & transgender people.* Campus Pride.

21. Tetreault, P. A., Fette, R., Meidlinger, P. C., & Hope, D. (2013). Perceptions of campus climate by sexual minorities. *Journal of Homosexuality*, 60(7), 947-964.

22. Vaccaro, A. (2012). Campus microclimates for LGBT faculty, staff, and students: An exploration of the intersections of social identity and campus roles. *Journal of Student Affairs Research and Practice*, 49(4), 429-446.

23. Woodford, M. R., Weber, G., Nicolazzo, Z., Hunt, R., Kulick, A., Coleman, T., & Renn, K. A. (2018). Depression and Attempted Suicide among LGBTQ College Students: Fostering Resilience to the Effects of Heterosexism and Cisgenderism on Campus. *Journal of College Student Development*, 59(4), 421-438.

24. Hayfield, N., Clarke, V., & Halliwell, E. (2014). Bisexual women's understandings of social marginalisation: "The heterosexuals don't understand us but nor do the

lesbians'. *Feminism & Psychology*, 24(3), 352–372. https://doi.org/10.1177/0959353514539651

25. Hemmings, C. (2002). *Bisexual spaces: A geography of sexuality and gender*. Psychology Press.

26. Maslach, C., Schaufeli, W. B., & Leiter, M. P. (2001). Job burnout. *Annual review of psychology*, 52(1), 397-422.

27. Gorski, P. C. (2015). Relieving burnout and the "Martyr Syndrome" among social justice education activists: the implications and effects of mindfulness. *The Urban Review*, 47(4), 696-716.

28. Gates, G. J. (2011). How many people are lesbian, gay, bisexual and transgender? Retrieved from https://escholarship.org/uc/item/09h684x2.pdf

Mysteries of Eros

1. Gadsby, Hannah. *Nanette*. Netflix. 2018.

Tapestries Woven in Many Threads

1. https://www.telegraph.co.uk/news/2018/05/31/bisexual-women-nearly-twice-likely-abused-partner/

2. https://www.hrc.org/resources/sexual-assault-and-the-lgbt-community

How Louisa May Alcott Helped Me to Survive Being Outed

1. Alcott, Louisa May. *Little Women*. London: Puffin, 2015. Print.

2. — *Good Wives*. London: Puffin, 1994. Print

3. — *Little Men*. London: Puffin, 1994. Print.

4. — *Jo's Boys*. London: Puffin, 1994. Print.

5. Showalter, Elaine. *Alternative Alcott*. New Brunswick: Rutgers

UP, 1997. Print.

6. *Legends of Tomorrow*. Perf. Caity Lotz. Berlanti Productions, DC Entertainment, Warner Bros. 2016. Television.

7. Boland, Eavan. *Collected Poems*. Manchester: Carcenet P, 1995. Print.

8. O'Connor, Sinéad. 'Nothing Compares 2 U.' *I Do Not Want What I Haven't Got*. Chrysalis. 1992. Cassette Tape.

SPECIAL THANKS

This book was made possible thanks to each and every one of our 293 donors on Kickstarter. We extend a massive thank you to all of you. We especially wanted to thank some standout folk below, along with those of our friends and professional peers who offered up their support and talent while we worked on the project. We couldn't have done this without your time and kindness. Thank you!

Ami Sommariva
Brenna Frederick
Cate Reed and Dan Walma
Chris Belous
Collin Knopp-Schwyn
Connor Grant Divers
Cordelia Sampson
David Rodemaker
Dustin Davis and Chloe Freeland
Ellie Dimopoulos

Eoghan Scott
Gay's the Word Bookshop
Gerry Desmond
Golden Hare Bookshop
Hannah Searle
Heather Pearson
Irina Preda
Jess Davis
John G. (Organiser, London Bisexuals Meetup Group)
Josie Deacon
Lighthouse Bookshop
Mairi Christine Oliver
Marit Mathisen
MaryMargaret
Media Diversified
Mervyn Galvin
Michaela Biggane, Jenny Jones and Esme Smithson
Mónica Martins
Peter Desmond
S. G. Davis
Sadie Wishart
Sarah Joy and Cameron
The OP Baker Family
Tom Hodges and Typewronger Bookshop
Twiggy the Cat
Vincent O'Brien
Will Osborn

MONSTROUS REGIMENT

Monstrous Regiment Publishing Ltd. is a small press based in a wee flat in Leith, Edinburgh, founded by two MSc Publishing graduates (Ellen Desmond and Lauren Nickodemus) while still at uni in 2017.

Their passion for publishing working class writers, as well as topics of intersectional feminism and sexuality led them on a mission to curate bold and fresh content; the stuff they felt was often missing from bookshelves.

In 2018 Monstrous expanded to include one contracted in-house designer (Hannah Killoh) and two student assistant interns (Lauren Mulvihill andd Kelli Staake).

MORE FROM MONSTROUS REGIMENT

Monstrous Regiment Literary Magazine is our feminist literary magazine featuring fiction, poetry, creative nonfiction, and visual arts led mainly by Scotland-based creatives.

Each issue of the magazine is themed around a certain colour, and all submissions are inspired in some way by the connotations that that colour might evoke or represent. This issue explores everything from IVF and post-apocalyptic worlds, to haunted forests and gardens of memory, to experiences in a mental hospital and the hype of big news. Featuring Kirsty Logan, Laura Clay, Elizabeth Sulis Kim, Claire Yspol, Angie Spoto, Sean Wai Keung and many more. *Emerald* is nature, nurture and everything in between...

PRAISE FOR THE BI-BLE VOL. 1

'There's not enough published on bisexual lives and experience in the UK. The Bi-ble was a welcome change and one of our bestsellers last year.' – Gay's The Word Bookshop

'[Crowdfunding's] potential for lifting marginalised voices into the spotlight is realised.' – *DIVA Magazine*

'If you're bisexual yourself, or just looking to learn more from others' lives, this is a great place to start.' – *CharlotteReadsThings*

'...carves out much-needed space to thoughtfully consider the bewildering and beautiful B in LGBTQ+.' – Emer O' Toole

'It's a crying shame to think that the LGBT+ community are silenced as frequently as they are, but what Monstrous Regiment are trying to do here is give a voice to bisexuals, and make other Beautiful Bis feel represented.' – *ANovelIdea*

'The essays in this collection are smart and informative, deeply personal, sometimes sad. The whole collection is ultimately celebratory and you put it down feeling free to be whoever you want to be, however you identify.'
– Rebecca Bonallie, Canongate Books

'One of the collection's strengths lies in its relatability for all readers, bi or not. Moments where biphobia is dissected, both in heterosexual and in lesbian and gay communities, are shrewd and unflinching but also appeal to these groups by being rooted in common experiences.'
– Becca Inglis, *The Wee Review*

'I think this is a great collection because it really shows the diversity within the community. It really shows the diversity of identities as well, in that, you can identify as bisexual and change your mind, or you can change your mind to identify as bisexual from something else and all of these things are valid and none of these things should be erased. It raises important points about the erasure of identities both within and without the LGBT community.' – Jen Gallagher

Monstrous
Regiment

@MonstrousRgmt
@MonstrousRgmt
facebook.com/MonstrousRgmt/

NOTES & THOUGHTS

These pages are for you to write down your notes and thoughts to make this book your own personal Bi-*ble*.